ROBERT SMITH SURTEES

By BONNIE RAYFORD NEUMANN

University of Wisconsin - Platteville

TWAYNE PUBLISHERS

A DIVISION OF G. K. HALL & CO., BOSTON

Copyright © 1978 by G. K. Hall & Co.

Published in 1978 by Twayne Publishers,
A Division of G. K. Hall & Co.
All Rights Reserved

Printed on permanent/durable acid-free paper and bound
in the United States of America

First Printing

823.8
S962 N
1978

Library of Congress Cataloging in Publication Data

Neumann, Bonnie Rayford.
Robert Smith Surtees.

(Twayne's English authors series ; TEAS 220)
Bibliography: p. 160 - 62
Includes index.
1.   Surtees, Robert Smith, 1805 - 1864
—Criticism and interpretation.
PR5499.S4Z6   823'.8   78-8062
ISBN 0-8057-6722-3

For George Hilliard

Contents

About the Author

Preface

Chronology

1. Robert Smith Surtees: Country Gentleman 13

2. The Jorrocks Trilogy 40

3. Tom Scott and Soapey Sponge 79

4. *Young Tom Hall* and the Fashionable Parodies 101

5. *Mr. Romford's Hounds: Mr. Sponge* Resumed 126

6. Surtees in Retrospect 143

Notes and References 152

Selected Bibliography 160

Index 163

About the Author

Bonnie Neumann, born and raised in Wisconsin, graduated with honors from the University of Wisconsin - Platteville with a major in English. She completed a Master of Fine Arts degree at the University of Iowa's Writers Workshop, where she studied with Nelson Algren, Kurt Vonnegut, Jr., and Vance Bourjaily. She went on to complete her Ph.D. in nineteenth-century English literature from the University of New Mexico with a dissertation on Mary Shelley which is soon to be published by the Salzburg Institute for English Language and Literature. She is also co-editing an anthology of world literature for Scribner's. Dr. Neumann is three-time winner of the Vinney Harvey creative-writing award, a recipient of the Bernice McNett award, and author of a short story, "Davey," published by *Mississippi Valley Writing*. She is currently Professor of English at the University of Wisconsin - Platteville, where she also serves as Department Chairman. In the spring of 1976 she was coordinator for a series of programs entitled "Change and the Problem of Equality for Women and Men Today," funded by a grant from the National Endowment for the Humanities. She is also active in such professional organizations as the American Association of University Professors, the Modern Language Association, the Association of University of Wisconsin Faculties, and the Coordinating Council for Women in Higher Education.

Preface

For a hundred years, from the middle of the nineteenth century to the middle of the twentieth, Robert Smith Surtees was known and read primarily by two groups of people, Victorian scholars and fox-hunters. In the last twenty-five years that has changed, for Surtees is now recognized by his small group of devoted admirers as much more than a mere "sporting novelist," a man who could write excitingly about a find, a chase, and a kill. Modern readers have discovered three more attributes in the writing of Surtees: he was one of the finest social historians of the early Victorian period; he created, much in the style of Dickens, dozens of charming and unforgettably eccentric characters; and he satirized in a way unmistakable and commendable the absurdities of society and human nature which he observed around him, universal absurdities which modern writers still satirize and modern readers still deplore.

The following analysis of Surtees's novels is intended to serve two purposes: first, to give those readers unfamiliar with his fiction sufficient information about those works to provide them with a basic understanding of the man and his writing, and, perhaps, to entice them to read *Handley Cross* or *Soapey Sponge* or *Mr. Romford;* and second, to analyze the individual novels of Surtees in terms of their satire, humor, characterization, theme, form, and social-historical value. In order to provide background for understanding the character of Surtees as well as to enumerate those incidents and experiences which either appeared directly in his novels or influenced his attitudes and, consequently, his satire, the first chapter is devoted to biographical information with emphasis on those points most relevant to Surtees as an author. The next four chapters take up the discussion of his novels one by one, providing enough information about the plot of each to enable the reader unfamiliar with that particular work to follow the critical discussion. The analyses are intended to show structural and thematic relationships between novels as well as to show Surtees's experimentation with literary forms and his growth as a writer. The final chapter summarizes the main points concerning Surtees as a novelist and a satirist, and contrasts Surtees's relationship with the critics and the reading public of his own day with the popularity and critical acclaim he has since received in the twentieth century.

BONNIE RAYFORD NEUMANN

University of Wisconsin - Platteville

Chronology

1805	Born May 17 at The Riding, Northumberland.
1806	Baptized in August at Bywell St. Andrew.
1812	Educated at Ovingham School, seven miles from the family estate of Hamsterley, County Durham.
1818	Enters Durham Grammar School.
1822	Articled to Mr. Robert Purvis, solicitor, of Newcastle-upon-Tyne.
1825	Articled to Mr. William Bell, solicitor, of London.
1828	Admitted to Chancery.
1829	Visits Brighton and Paris, and owns his first pack of hounds jointly with Colonel Charitée at Boulogne.
1830	Employed as hunting correspondent for the *Sporting Magazine*, his first article, "Breaking Ground," appearing in February.
1831	Establishes and edits the *New Sporting Magazine* in conjunction with publisher Rudolph Ackermann. Starts writing the Jorrocks stories. *The Horseman's Manual* published. Brother Anthony dies, leaving Robert heir to Hamsterley.
1836	Resigns editorship of the *New Sporting Magazine* and retires to Hamsterley.
1837	Mother dies. Runs for Parliament as Conservative; withdraws before election.
1838	Father, Anthony, dies, making Robert Squire of Hamsterley. *Jorrocks' Jaunts and Jollities* published, a collection of earlier-published Jorrocks stories.
1841	Married May 29 to Elizabeth Jane Fenwick, daughter of Addison Fenwick, J. P., of Field House and Pallion Hall.
1842	Appointed Deputy Lieutenant and Justice of the Peace for Durham County.
1843	*Handley Cross* published in book form after running in considerably different form as serial in *New Sporting Magazine*.
1844	Appointed Major of Durham Militia. Joins

Northumberland Society for the Protection of British Agriculture and becomes active against repeal of Corn Laws.

1845   *Hillingdon Hall* published in book form after first twenty-two chapters appeared from February 1843 to June 1844 in the *New Sporting Magazine*.

1846   *The Analysis of the Hunting Field* published from articles written for *Bell's Life* from October 1845 to April 1846.

1847   *Hawbuck Grange* published after running as serial in *Bell's Life* starting in 1846.

1849   *Mr. Sponge's Sporting Tour* published in serial form in the *New Monthly Magazine;* runs from January 1849 to April 1851.

1851   *Young Tom Hall* runs in the *New Monthly Magazine* from October 1851 to January 1853, when, as a result of argument with editor Ainsworth, publication stopped and the novel was never completed.

1852   Conceives the idea for the *Field*, undertakes a hunting tour to help fill pages of its early editions, and serves as chief correspondent for its first issues.

1853   *Mr. Sponge's Sporting Tour* published in book form with illustrations by John Leech.

1854   *Handley Cross* republished with illustrations by Leech.

1856   Appointed High Sheriff of Durham County. Edits a new edition of Blaine's *Encyclopaedia of Rural Sports*.

1857   *Ask Mamma* issued by Bradbury and Evans in thirteen monthly parts; published in book form with Leech illustrations in 1858.

1858   *Plain or Ringlets* issued by Bradbury and Evans in thirteen monthly parts; published in book form with Leech illustrations in 1860.

1861   Unpublished "Description of Durham" written.

1864   Dies March 16 at Brighton. Buried at Ebchester. *Mr. Romford's Hounds* issued by Bradbury and Evans in twelve monthly parts; published in book form in 1865.

1924   E. D. Cuming edits Surtees's previously unpublished memoirs under the title *Robert Smith Surtees, Creator of "Jorrocks" by Himself and E. D. Cuming*.

CHAPTER 1

Robert Smith Surtees:
Country Gentleman

IN these days of stress and change it is becoming more and more difficult to realize the undisturbed seclusion, the unruffled serenity, of the lives of men who led the same existence as their fathers had done before them for centuries, whose ancestors had differed from themselves more in clothes than in mind, to whom change meant little more than the addition of a wing to the old manor, an experiment in field drainage, or, more commonly, the acquisition of another family portrait, gazing in undiminished serenity from the oak-panelled dining-hall upon its descendants."[1] This was the life into which Robert Smith Surtees was born, and, with the exception of sixteen years between the ages of fifteen and thirty-one, this was the life he lived. Just one characteristic set him apart from the rest of his class of country squires—he had what he called a "taste for scribbling."[2] This inclination was to make him one of England's finest satirists and social commentators, and, without question, England's greatest sporting novelist.

I Early Years

Robert Surtees was born on May 17, 1805, one of nine children, and spent his early years in the secluded and secure environment of his family's estate of Hamsterley, County Durham. "It was a typical nineteenth-century squire's home, a background of hounds and horses, port and claret, game and beef-steaks, country sport and country duties."[3] It was an agreeable and congenial life. As Surtees describes it in his novel *Plain or Ringlets*, "A Country house in former days was little better than a great unlicensed inn—everything was taken in that arrived, and everybody had to be refreshed that came."[4]

Apart from the general life-style of Hamsterley, little is known of
Surtees's early life except that, at a young age, he joined his father
in the hunting field. It is difficult now to appreciate the importance
of fox-hunting to the people of that day and, especially, of that
locality. County Durham is located in the far north of England in
the rough "hill country." The climate is unpredictable, the
summers frequently cold and wet, and the winters characterized by
frost, snow, and occasional tempest. In those days before the
railroad, small farming communities were almost totally isolated by
bad roads and bad weather. Surtees's description of his own trip
from Hamsterley to London by coach in 1825 is fatiguing even to
read. "I travelled up from Newcastle-on-Tyne by the old Highflyer
coach, to catch which at eight o'clock in the morning I had to leave
Hamsterley between five and six. Then, by a steady persevering
grind continued throughout all that day, all that night, and all the
following day, we reached the dismal White Horse in Fetter Lane at
eight that night. The fare was £6 inside, and it was considered very
fine travelling."[5] "In truth," he confesses in *Plain or Ringlets*, "the
country gentlemen were a land-locked, leg-tied tribe. . . . There
was no running up to town for a week in those days. It took the best
part of a week coming from a remote country to make the journey
and recover from the effects of it."[6]

Consequently, such communities had to depend upon their own
resources for entertainment. The demands of farming kept people
occupied through the spring, summer, and autumn, but the winters
were given over to socializing, and the hunting field frequently
formed the center of social life. Three days a week the local squire
and farmers and farmhands would be joined by hunting enthusiasts
from as far away as thirty miles. Such a gathering provided more
than the excitement of the hunt—it was the primary means of com-
munication between people of different occupations and social
classes. In *Plain or Ringlets* Surtees explains the importance of
hunting to country communities like his own in Durham County.

If there were no other argument in favour of field-sports than the sociality
they engender, it would be amply sufficient to carry them through. Contrast a country house, from which there is hunting or shooting, with one
where there is nothing to do, and there will not be much doubt about the
matter. The sporting furnishes the chief dish in the bill of fare, and with
plenty of good exercise, a good appetite, and good spirits, are sure to be
engendered. If there is nothing to do—nothing but eat, eat, eat, a man had
better pen himself up in a club, and be stall-fed like an ox. Field-sports
should, therefore, be encouraged by every legitimate means.[7]

"We consider the maintenance of field sports of immense importance to the well-being of a country," he continues in his *Analysis of the Hunting Field*. "They not only engender a fine manly daring spirit . . . but they materially tend to promote a healthy spirit of sociality and intercourse among neighbors."[8] Hunting, then, had become more than entertainment; it was a valuable, democratic, social institution.

The hunting which Surtees did as a boy had a profound effect on his attitude toward the sport, for he developed a respect for hunting and its serious participants that is obvious in every one of his novels. His father, who kept packs of both fox-hounds and harriers, was an excellent sportsman and an ideal example of a country gentleman. Charles Apperley, better known as "Nimrod," visited Hamsterley in 1834 and wrote the following description of Anthony Surtees:

Now the 'Squire of Hamsterley is . . . . "every inch of him" a sportsman . . . he being a most religious observer of the remains of ancient times, in the unbounded hospitality of his house and table . . . in short, a true sample of the old English 'Squire, and as good a judge of a horse, a hound, a bottle of port wine, and an oak-tree, as any man in England, or any where else . . . who receives under the shadow of his roof, not only his friends themselves, but their servants, their horses, their *hounds*—in short any thing they may favour him with, that contributes to their amusement and comfort. He has, however, an excellent house to stow them in, and perhaps one of the best timbered estates in the county of Durham, in the management of which . . . he is said to have few equals.[9]

In addition to hunting with his father's hounds, the young Surtees also had experience with the neighboring pack of Mr. Ralph Lambton, Member of Parliament for Durham City and Master of Fox-Hounds for over forty years. Under the guidance of these two men Surtees learned the craft well. He discovered that the true value of hunting lay in training the hounds and watching them work, not in flamboyant races at breakneck speed across open country. He realized that the true sportsman was willing to travel long, boring miles on dreary days in order to sit on horseback for hours while the hounds searched futilely for the fox, and then, for pure love of the sport, come back again two days later to do the same. He formed his ideal master of hounds based on Lambton, a man of complete integrity, high principle, and dedication to the welfare of his constituents. Surtees wrote a description of Mr. Lambton which survives as part of his unpublished "Description of Durham" written in 1861. "Ralph Lambton was, indeed, a model master, a model man—just the sort of character for youth to be taught to look up to as a perfect specimen of a highly-polished English gentleman—so courteous, so considerate, so alive to all the little delicacies by which pleasure is conferred or pain excited; above all, so truly honourable in his conduct, and sincere and faithful in his friendships."[10] Those early experiences established these ideals so strongly in him that for the rest of his life any deviation from them was to arouse his unmitigated scorn and inspire his most bitter satire.

Surtees's formal education began at Ovingham, a private school about seven miles from Hamsterley. He himself confesses that "here formerly many of the aristocracy of the North received the rudiments of their education."[11] Those "rudiments" were probably similar to the curriculum of most boys' schools of the day, described by Leonard Cooper as "the classics before everything, a lot of scripture and a little mathematics, a liberal use of the birch and anything but a liberal supply of food."[12] One thing is certain: Ovingham's being so near Hamsterley made it possible for him to return home often and continue his hunting.

There is, however, one detail of his life at Ovingham that deserves further consideration, for it illustrates a major aspect of his future writing, his inclination to base his fictional characters upon real people with whom he was personally acquainted. Already Surtees had developed the ability to observe people and file away their characters for future use. No better example of this tendency can be found than in the appearance of his eccentric Ovingham schoolmaster, the Reverend James Birkett, as Mr. Jogglebury Crowdey in the novel *Mr. Sponge's Sporting Tour*. Describing Mr. Birkett, Surtees writes in his memoirs that "he had the most ludicrous propensity for making and hoarding up walking-sticks that ever was heard of. He could not see or hear of a promising sapling but that he would be at it and, having converted it into a walking-stick, would add it to his already redundant collection. Every garret and spare place about the house was full of them: they must have been counted by thousands. . . . I firmly believe that he thought he was amassing a fortune for his successors therewith."[13] Forty years later Jogglebury Crowdey in *Mr. Sponge*, "being a great man for what he called gibbey-sticks, hunted for the purpose of finding them . . . he generally appeared at large woodlands into which he would ride with the hounds . . . making observations all the while of the hazels and the hollies, and the blackthorns . . . that he thought would fashion into curious-handled walking-sticks. . . . At the time of which we are writing, he had accumulated a vast quantity—thousands . . . and as he cut, and puffed, and wheezed, and modelled . . . he chuckled and thought how well he was providing for his family."[14] An earlier novel, *Hillingdon Hall,* presents still another character who might well have been based on Mr. Birkett. In that novel the schoolmaster, Mr. Slooman, "being on the best terms with himself, coughed and hemmed and stroked his chin, and looked complacently around, as much as to say, 'I am Sir Oracle, and when I ope my lips let no dog bark.' He was a little, bristly-headed, badger-eyed, pedantic, radical school-master."[15] Surtees has been accused by Mr. Cooper of having more talent for observation than for imagination,[16] and his flagrant use of actual people of his acquaintance as characters for his novels would seem to add credence to the charge. But one must remember that he was a "satirist of character types rather than individuals," as Susan Hallgarth points out in her dissertation on Surtees, "so that when he did model his characters on actual people he focused on them as representatives of a type rather than as individuals."[17] But however he may have exaggerated his characters for the sake of caricature, their basic outline came from real people and real life.

In 1818, at the age of thirteen, Surtees left Ovingham to enroll in Durham Grammar School. Little record remains of that part of his life; all that is known for certain is that in 1822, according to the Law Society's records, he was articled, or apprenticed, to Mr. Robert Purvis, a solicitor in Newcastle-upon-Tyne, the largest city in the vicinity of Hamsterley. Most Surtees biographers have assumed that Surtees left Durham Grammar School after only one year, and, because no record of his life between 1819 and 1822 exists, they speculate that he must have worked for Mr. Purvis during those three years before becoming formally articled. However, Mr. David Johnston-Jones reveals that the *Register of Durham School* records that an R. S. Surtees left.there in 1819 and also that an R. Surtees left in December 1821. Since it is unlikely that those entries refer to two different people, it is quite possible that Surtees spent those mysterious three years studying quietly at Durham School.[18] In any event, by 1822 Surtees had begun the study of law.

II *Law: Newcastle and London*

Surtees's choice of the law as a career was a natural one. He was a second son; as such, he could have had no reasonable expectation of inheriting the family estate. Only a limited number of professions were open to one of his class and background, primarily armed service, religious vocation, or law. Judging from his satire, his presentation of Colonel Blunt and the Heaveysteed Dragoons[19] for example, he must have had little respect for armed service, and there is no indication in any of his writings or in any record of his life that he was particularly religious. The elimination of those options left the law as the almost inevitable choice. But "to speak of the Law as a career for him is probably incorrect," surmises Leonard Cooper. "It was at most a gentlemanly way of passing time and acquiring useful knowledge until he should either return to Hamsterley or to some other estate, there to hunt, to administer justice and live the life of his forbears. He does not seem to have regarded it himself in the light of a career nor to have taken any interest in it."[20] As Mr. Cuming puts it, "We glean enough from his own writings and papers to assure us that he did not suffer legal pursuits to interfere seriously with his enjoyment of life."[21] While at Newcastle that "enjoyment of life" definitely included getting home as often as possible for those all-important hunts.

The normal term for a law apprenticeship was five years, and in 1825, according to the Law Society's records, Surtees was "further articled" to Mr. William Bell of London. Now, for the first time, he was far enough from home to have a degree of independence. But the change was to be far from revolutionary. At the age of twenty his ideas and attitudes had already been established. "The ideas and convictions that had already been formed in the young Surtees were to stay with him all his life. It had been a sheltered life so far—home and school, hunting and country. He had not even had the chance of encountering new ideas and different types that a public school and university might have given him. . . . He started on this journey to London knowing, surely, as little of the world as any young hero of a fairy-tale setting off to make his fortune."[22] Although he was to travel widely, covering much of England as a hunting correspondent and even venturing into France, nothing he saw or did seemed to alter that fundamental Hamsterley character or those ideals of gentlemanly conduct and sportsmanship based on his observations of his father and Ralph Lambton.

Surtees evidently took the study of law even less seriously in London than he had done in Newcastle, for his memoirs make almost no mention of it. But those experiences were not wasted; they were to provide him with one of his most successful satirical subjects. He writes in *Plain or Ringlets* of three kinds of lawyers: "able, unable, and lamentable."[23] In *Ask Mamma* he describes a law office: "all is dull, solemn, and dry—paper, paper, paper—a redundancy of paper."[24] His description of magistrates in *Hillingdon Hall* is barbed indeed. "If a man goes into Guildhall . . . he cannot help being struck with the resemblance there is among the loose, purple-robed, white-faced, flabby, live-turtle-looking things ranged on each side of the chair, called Aldermen or Common Councilmen."[25] In *Handley Cross* a law student named Charley Stobbs is articled to a Mr. Twister. Knowing Surtees's preference for writing from his own life, Stobbs's experiences could very well have been those of the author.

Mr. Twister was one of those legal nuisances called conveyancers, whom it is to be hoped some contrivance will be found to extinguish, and he could find a loop-hole for an unwilling purchaser to creep out of in the very best of titles. Having plenty to do himself, he took as many pupils as ever he could get, to help each other to do nothing. Each of these paid him a hundred guineas a year, in return for which they had the run of a dingy, carpetless room, the use of some repulsive-looking desks, and the liberty to copy twenty volumes of manuscript precedents, that the great Mr. Twister had copied himself when a pupil with great Mr. Somebody-else.[26]

Stobbs, probably like Surtees, was strongly tempted to give up the study of law because, he says, its "crotchety quibbles are enough to disgust any one with a taste for truth."[27]

But the center of Surtees's attention during those years was still the hunting field, and in London he encountered a kind of hunting quite different from that found at Hamsterley. For this was the area of popular subscription packs, each headed by a professional master of hounds with a professional staff and supported through "subscriptions" from all those people, from any walk of life, regardless of social position or financial condition, who, for whatever reason, wanted to hunt. Every Saturday the parade of sportsmen, "the merchant on his hunter, the butcher on his cob, the tinker on his donkey,"[28] and foot-people in abundance trailed out of London and headed for the open fields. In *Jorrocks' Jaunts and Jollities* Surtees asks, "What true-bred city sportsman has not in his

day put off the most urgent business—perhaps his marriage, or even
the interment of his rib—that he might 'brave the morn' with that
renowned pack, the Surrey subscription fox-hounds." "Who can
wonder," he continues, "that smoke-dried cits, pent up all week,
should gladly fly from their shops to enjoy a day's sport on a Saturday?"[29] It was to these people, London-bred, hard-working, striving
to enlarge their lives beyond their store-counters and their worlds
beyond the borders of London, that the term "Cockney" came to
be applied. To many people, especially those of rural England, the
Cockney was a joke. And, when it came to hunting and
horsemanship, he certainly was an amateur. "The furthest removed,
whether in station or in location, like to know how the Londoners
proper live—how and where they ride, fish, shoot—above all,
whereabouts, and after what fashion, they *hunt*," exclaimed J. G.
Lockhart in the Cockneys' defense in an 1843 *Quarterly Review* article on *Handley Cross*. "Still there has always been an unworthy
leaning to disparage and ridicule the prowess of the East; as if it
were not hard enough in all conscience for people to be cooped up
in bricks and mortar all the year, without having the slow-pointing
finger of scorn proclaiming them cockneys whenever they venture
forth for a breath of fresh air. 'The unkindest cut of all' is, that city
sportsmen are mainly indebted to city pencils and city pens for this
unenviable notoriety."[30]

Surtees, too, defended the Cockneys, but in a different way and
for different reasons than did Mr. Lockhart. He praised their hunting. He saw men inspired by the love of hunting as he was inspired.
He felt the same warm glow of camaraderie that pervaded the most
distinguished hunts. He frequently saw, in the handling of hounds
and horses, genuine expertise. And he came to the defense of those
hunts in both his nonfiction and his fiction, his *Hunting Tours* and
his Jorrocks trilogy. The highest tribute he could have paid them he
rendered in the character of John Jorrocks, greengrocer and tea-
dealer, the epitome of Cockney temperament, whom he elevates in
Handley Cross to the esteemed position of Master of Fox-Hounds.
"A natural born sportsman, his lot being cast behind a counter instead of in the country, is one of those frolics of fortune that there is
no accounting for. To remedy the error of the blind goddess, Mr.
Jorrocks had taken to hunting as soon as he could keep a horse, and
though his exploits were long confined to the suburban county of
Surrey, he should rather be 'credited' for keenness in following the
sport . . . than 'debited' as a Cockney and laughed at for his
pains."[31] Mr. Noakes correctly states that "it is quite a mistake and

a misreading of the novels to imagine that Surtees meant us to laugh at the idea of a grocer like Jorrocks going out to hunt. He saw nothing odd or preposterous about it."[32] In *Hillingdon Hall* Surtees even permits Jorrocks to rise to Justice of the Peace and Member of Parliament.

In 1828 Surtees was admitted to Chancery, and the goal of six years was accomplished. Now he had leisure time and, if he felt somewhat at "loose-ends" concerning his future, he gave no indication of it. He set out to enjoy himself, which, for him, meant that he set out to hunt. He traveled first to Brighton, one of the many "watering-places" which had sprung up during the eighteenth century to "minister quite frankly to scandal and gout."[33] Such areas as Brighton and Shotley Bridge not only served Surtees well as settings for his novels, but also presented him with a seemingly endless parade of colorful characters who eventually ended up virtually undisguised between the covers of his books. For instance, there was the Master of the South Down pack, a Colonel Windham, who controlled his hounds with a whistle, "a peculiar method," Surtees comments, "the like of which I have never seen before and have never seen since."[34] In *Hawbuck Grange,* written seventeen years later, Captain Cashbox controls his hounds with a whistle.[35] In *Handley Cross* is found another example in the character of Captain Doleful, based on a colorful Captain Eld, Brighton's self-appointed "Master of Ceremonies."[36] Perhaps the most amusing of all was Baron Gablenz from Saxony, a young man who prowled Brighton in search of an heiress to marry. "You have nothing to do but tell the Baron that so-and-so had money and he would be at her in a moment."[37] Gablenz was extremely fond of what he called "foxin' " and made a reputation by wearing outlandish clothes on the hunting field. He makes a brief appearance in *Hawbuck Grange* as the Prince of Spankenhausen[38] and, twelve years later, is more fully developed in *Plain or Ringlets* as Prince Pirouetteza, still extravagantly dressed, still looking for an heiress, and still, after a fashion, "foxin'."[39]

Wishing to enjoy his new liberty to the fullest, Surtees decided in 1829 to cross over into France. He went first to Paris and then to Boulogne, where he had a series of adventures so preposterous[40] that he was soon driven home again, shaking his head over the absurdity of Frenchmen and sharpening his prejudice against all foreigners, prejudice that, unfortunately, reveals itself several times in his novels.

When Surtees returned from France he was twenty-four years old

and in search of a new career. The practice of law held no attrac-
tion. During the winter of 1829, the cold weather making hunting
impossible, he started writing what he called a "semi-sporting"
novel. This was an entirely original idea, for he claims in his
memoirs that "up to that time no one had ever essayed to anything
in the sporting line that he was not prepared to swear to."[41] Sporting fiction, then, was virtually unknown until invented by Surtees.
When the novel was about two-thirds completed he showed it to
two of his friends who "so laughed it to scorn that I put it on the
fire, and half resolved to abandon the pursuit of letters for the
future."[42] Fortunately his "taste for scribbling" overcame his
halfhearted resolution and he was soon launched on a literary
career.

III   *Hunting Correspondent and Editor*

The art of using hounds to hunt fox, hare, and deer dates from
antiquity, but the sport reached a level of popularity in England
between 1820 and 1870 to which no other sport to this date has
come close. "Sport, from being merely a hearty pastime, had
become a ritual as well," explains Frederick Darton. "It had
superseded coaching as a subject of wagers, and was becoming
refined."[43] So important did it become to English society that even
nonparticipants demanded details of the latest hunt and the latest
hunting gossip. This demand, coupled with the sportsmen's natural
delight in reading about themselves, led to a new literary form, the
monthly sporting magazine. Appropriately, the foremost of these
was entitled the *Sporting Magazine*. It was to the editor of this
publication, Mr. Shury, that Surtees presented his next literary effort, a few scenes he had sketched from his personal hunting journal. "The bait took," he writes, "and I presently found myself installed as first fiddle in the hunting line."[44] His timing was fortunate. Until 1830 the chief hunting correspondent for *Sporting* had
been Charles James Apperley, the same "Nimrod" who furnished
the description of Surtees's father and Hamsterley. But just before
Surtees's association with the magazine Nimrod and his employers
had disagreed about that inevitable problem of a raise in salary, and
Nimrod had quit the magazine. Surtees was installed in Nimrod's
place, publishing his first article, "Breaking Ground," in February
1830, an article dealing with "the propriety of digging a fox when
he has gone to ground in a covered watercourse whence he cannot

be bolted."[45] He signed the paper "A Durham Spokesman" and thus initiated his lifelong habit of anonymous authorship.

For the next two seasons Surtees roamed the country visiting various estates and reporting under the pseudonym "Nim South" on the quality of all kinds of hunts. "This was the life in which he revelled," writes Mr. Cuming, "and his accounts of his journeyings and the sport he enjoyed are full of zest."[46] During the summer he took part in the nonhunting activities reflected in the Jorrocks stories: traveling to Brighton and Paris, racing at Newmarket, boating on the Thames.

In temperament and interests he was entirely different from his predecessor. Nimrod was almost unbearably egotistical; when he attended a hunt it was his expectation that he, not the fox, would be the center of attention. Surtees, by contrast, had no interest in advertising his presence at a hunt; he usually sent his horse on ahead and traveled by coach, preferring to stay not with the local squire but rather at the local inn. Nimrod's primary interest at a hunt was not so much the hunt itself as the famous people who attended it. "His tours were a triumphant procession from mansion to mansion, and his articles were lit up, as stars light the heavens, by clusters of anecdotes of peers and great Masters and famous men across a country . . . the period gossip of English and Scottish country seats."[47] Surtees, on the other hand, found "his attention . . . directed to the way hounds were hunted and stuck to their fox far more than to such incidents as Lord Cutemdown taking a toss into a brook."[48] "Whilst Nimrod trains his bemused optics on the lords and the fashionables in the field," writes Aubrey Noakes, "Surtees is keeping an alert eye open to expose every rheumy-eyed, unshaven horse-coper-looking fraud in sight."[49] Watson goes so far as to say of him, "A weakness in Surtees as a critic of hunting lay in his finnickiness. He had as many prejudices as a fussy old lady. He looked at a huntsman's boots before his face, at the way he used his voice or horn rather than whether he killed his fox."[50] Surtees was certainly aware of such criticism, for in his novel *Hawbuck Grange* he defends his methods. "We may observe how much better it is for a respectable paper to have a regular cut-along correspondent, who sticks to the truth, and tells what he sees, calling things by their proper names—fools, fools—humbugs, humbugs—and so on, instead of one of your word-sprawling gentry, who are perfectly bewildered when they come to handle a hunt, and only make absurdity more ridiculous."[51]

In other words, Surtees, at age twenty-five, was already applying in his nonfictional articles those same standards to the art of hunting that were to dominate his novels for the next thirty-three years. To look at the scene of the hunt in Surtees's writings merely as a convenient setting for his action is to read his novels as mere sporting chronicles, quite missing the satirical point. "For him hunting was a touchstone for men of character, of simplicity, honesty, and fair-play,"[52] writes Susan Hallgarth, and Mr. Watson elaborates: "Fox-hunting provided in his particular angle of satire a new arena for the ancient human by-play of hypocrisy."[53] Surtees himself explains how this aspect of his satire is to be interpreted, for he claims in his *Analysis of the Hunting Field* that he has never known "any man worthy the name of sportsman, who was not a good fellow."[54] How does one tell a "good fellow" from the not-so-good fellows? By the way he dresses, explains Surtees, and by his aristocratic air and his concern for his horse and, especially, by his motivation for hunting. "We can tell a fox-hunter almost at a glance—a real one, we mean," he explains in *Town and Country Papers*. "There is a nice, neat, quiet, easy manner about him."[55] If he hunts solely for love of sport rather than to sell a horse or impress a lady, to wear a red coat or to fulfill his duty, then he is a "good fellow." "Happy are they who go out to please themselves, and not to astonish others,"[56] he declares in *Mr. Romford's Hounds*. Then, if the sportsman rides to spare his horse, neither afraid to take jumps or swim rivers when necessary nor ashamed to take advantage of a convenient gate or a break in a hedge, then he is a "good fellow." If his dress and demeanor are appropriate to the time and place in which he finds himself, "the essence of common sense and practicality,"[57] then he is a "good fellow." One such "good fellow" is Facey Romford: "He was most assiduous in showing sport, no day being too long or distance too great for him; and he rode in a way that astonished the natives, saving his horse where saving was right, but never saving him to the detriment of sport. . . . He never turned away from anything, and if he couldn't leap he would lead over, his only anxiety being to get to his hounds."[58]

"Now what we feel about Surtees," Moira O'Neill explains, "is that being a natural man himself, he understood the nature of sport and the hearts of sportsmen as no one ever yet has understood them. A man who will hunt with hounds if he can, and if he can't do that will hunt with ferrets, and if he can't do that will hunt a rat in a rickyard rather than not hunt at all,—that is the kind of sportsman whom Surtees honoured."[59] Next to his few "good fellows" Surtees parades a collection of blackguards, hypocrites, swells, gulls, weaklings, braggarts, horse-dealers, thieves, gamblers, drunkards, con-men, and phonies that absolutely staggers the imagination. "What Watson terms Surtees's 'finnickiness,'" argues Ms. Hallgarth, "is suggestive of his satiric attitude, his perception and presentation of the outward man—his horses and hounds, dress and habits—as representative of inner character."[60]

This delineation of character type, this contrast between the few natural "good fellows" and society's vast majority of hypocrites and dandies, is the basis of Surtees's satire, and his methods and motives remain the same when in later novels he moves away from the hunting field into country-house society. Those articles for the *Sporting Magazine* were extremely important for the young writer, for although, "because of his insistence on criticism—and hence on instruction—rather than praise," they sometimes "acted as burrs in the side of sportsmen,"[61] he did establish in them the groundwork for all his later novels, taking his satirical stance, as it were. His basic attitudes and ideals never changed, for additional experience meant for him merely a greater selection of materials with which to paint over and over again, from different perspectives and in different hues, that same picture of personal and social hypocrisy and absurdity.

Even his famous predecessor, the egotistical Nimrod, became a target for Surtees's satire, for the young journalist believed the older man and his aristocratic cronies to be perverting the spirit of the hunt for their own selfish ends. For example, he presented Nimrod as the "swell" in his story "The Swell and the Surrey," a dandy who had "just turned out of the hands of his valet, and presents the very *beau ideal* of his caste—'quite the lady,' in fact."[62] He made fun of Nimrod's writing style when he introduced him as "Mr. H'Apperley Nimrod" in "Mr. Jorrocks' Dinner Party." His final unquestionable portrayal of Nimrod was as Pomponious Ego in *Handley Cross*. That presentation was so blatant that the *Quarterly*, in its review of the novel, warned Surtees to "curb his propensity to caricature"[63] and the *Times* described the character as "highly coloured" but "utterly unmistakable."[64] It took Surtees a while to learn to disguise his feelings behind characters less clearly identifiable, to elevate his satire from the personal to the general, but when he learned that lesson, he learned it well.

It is ironic that, different though Nimrod and Surtees were, both men parted with the *Sporting Magazine* over the question of money. Up to this time Surtees had evidently been traveling for the magazine at his own expense, receiving payment for his articles, it is true, but payment which was not sufficient to reimburse his expenses. "None save those who have tried it can have any idea of the enormous cost of hunting touring," he remarks.[65] Early in 1831 he approached the editor for a share in the magazine. He had supplied five articles and been asked to do a sixth, and he simply wanted to receive what he considered to be fair pay for his labors. His request was denied, even though, as the editor informed him, the proprietors "were perfectly aware of the value of his services" and were willing to make him an offer "greater than the proprietors ever intended to make, and more than under any circumstances would ever be made to any other gentleman."[66] Whatever offers they made were obviously not sufficient, however, for in February of that year he left the *Sporting Magazine* and struck out on his own.

Surtees had recently met the publisher Rudolph Ackermann, and the two men formed a partnership and began publishing their own magazine, with Surtees as editor, called the *New Sporting Magazine*. They advertised it as a periodical "established by gentlemen who carried it on more for amusement than profit."[67] Fortunately, for the next five years, the *New Sporting* provided Surtees not only with both amusement and profit, but with experience and a literary reputation as well. "He has written of every kind of run, in every sort of country, upon every kind of horse that the experience of ten ordinary men would include."[68] In addition to his own work, he managed to solicit articles from some of the best writers of the day, and even coaxed the celebrated academician Abraham Cooper away from the "old" *Sporting*. The new magazine "was a great success, and for the duration of Surtees's interest in it effectively held pride of place in the hunting lodges of the gentry over the publication it had been set up to oust."[69] It was also the perfect apprenticeship for his career: it taught him, through experience, what the public wanted and what it would not accept; it gave him an opportunity to sharpen his satirical wit; it made his name known and his talent respected; and it encouraged the creation of John Jorrocks, Surtees's most famous literary character. Jorrocks first appeared in the third issue of the magazine and, "for the next fourteen years," Mr. Cooper writes, "he was never long absent from his creator's mind. From July 1831 to September 1834 he riots through the pages of the *New Sporting Magazine*, hunting, shooting, racing, masquerading as a French colonel, and, as ever, reveling in good food and good drink."[70] "The most useful man to the work beyond all question," Surtees himself admits, "was Mr. Jorrocks, the sporting grocer of Great Coram Street, who not only followed all legitimate field sports, but indulged in diverse vagaries not connected therewith. Jorrocks could turn his hand to almost anything." He goes on to say prophetically that Jorrocks "soon 'took,' and has ever since remained a fixture with the sporting world."[71] The Jorrocks sketches were later revised and published in book form as *Jorrocks' Jaunts and Jollities*, the first novel of the Jorrocks trilogy.

In addition to his magazine, Surtees published during this period another work which enhanced his literary and sporting reputation, the nonfictional *Horseman's Manual*. It is a book of little interest to nonhorsemen, and Mr. E. D. Cuming provides an idea of its contents. "It describes and considers a number of cases which had come before the courts, gives judicial decisions, expert opinions and usages in connection with sale and purchase, privately and by auction."[72] It seems that Surtees may have derived some real benefit from copying those "twenty volumes of manuscript precedents" he complains about in *Handley Cross*. Besides, as Mr. Noakes affirms, the book "is enlivened more than legal textbooks commonly are by a number of anecdotes about horse-copers; their wiles, dodges, and stratagems."[73] This work could well have sparked the interest that led Surtees many years later to write *Mr. Sponge's Sporting Tour* about just such a "horse-coper."

"Editing is very good fun—for a time,"[74] Surtees once wrote, and in 1836, after five years with the *New Sporting*, he resigned from the magazine. "For some time past circumstances have prevented our giving the work the attention which it requires,"[75] he explains in his "Farewell," and considering the demands of his personal life at that time his reason was certainly valid. His older brother, Anthony, had died of smallpox in 1831, leaving Surtees heir to Hamsterley. His mother and father were both in failing health and he was forced to assume more and more of the duties connected with the estate. He took these responsibilities seriously, and soon realized that the demands of editorship, which included living in London, and the traveling necessitated by his hunting tours interfered with his trips to Hamsterley. By 1835 he must have had a clear idea of his priorities, for that was the first year he failed to renew the annual certificate necessary for the practice of law. In

1836, with no sign of regret, he left London and retired, permanently, to the family estate. At the age of thirty-two he slipped quietly back into that slow pace of life and those quiet country concerns that had dominated the lives of his father and grandfather before him.

IV   *Country Gentleman*

He had chosen his career and he was fortunate in it. He cared for two things, hunting and writing; and for the rest of his life he was to combine the two . . . he was able to make a living—in so far as he needed to make a living—out of his pleasures. In nearly every way his was to be a life free from the ordinary cares and struggles, from financial anxiety and from insecurity of every sort. . . . What he was when he began to write at the age of twenty-four he remained to the end—a country gentleman, a hunting man, withdrawn and aloof from the turmoil of the world; satisfied with his own surroundings, a little intolerant and contemptuous of any other world than his own; incurious about the problems of his day, indifferent to social and industrial change, kindly, arrogant and obstinate. This, combined with a sense of humour that was often unkind and never subtle, was the equipment with which he began his literary career.[76]

"He was a plain well-educated Englishman," says Mr. Darton, "with a high sense of duty, and deep inherent love of the country, and much more than the average share of brains."[77] One year after his return to Hamsterley Surtees's mother died, and before the next year was over his father, too, was dead. In 1838 he became Squire of Hamsterley.

The only available physical description of the young Surtees is the one recorded on his passport in August 1835: "Age, 30 years; Height, 6 feet 1 inch; Hair, Brown; Forehead, Wide; Eyes, Brown; Nose, Ordinary; Beard, Chestnut; Face, Oval; Girth, Average."[78] He was fond of good clothes; in the habit of considering clothes to be a barometer of character, he was determined to dress well himself. In other areas of life he was quiet and reserved. Despite the emphasis in his novels on food and drink he was personally moderate in both.

He was, however, acutely conscious of his social position and, as his scathing satire of foolish and self-serving country gentry so clearly illustrates, he guarded closely the dignity which that position afforded. One incident from his personal life illustrates well the code of honor by which he lived and against which he measured all other men, the code of his forefathers, the code that had been demonstrated to him as a boy by his father and Ralph Lambton. In 1838 Surtees was made the object of offensive remarks written by J. W. Carleton in the *Sporting Magazine.* His first thought was to challenge the offender to a duel. He hesitated only because he doubted whether Carleton was considered gentleman enough to deserve the honor; after all, one does not lower oneself by dueling with those below one's social class. His doubts were confirmed when a friend assured him that Carleton had offended Mr. Greville in the same manner, but Greville "never for a moment thought of fighting him, which, if he had considered him a gentleman he would, of course have done." He went on to assure Surtees that "this sets your question at rest. If Greville never could for a moment think of fighting him, I don't see how you can."[79] "It must be allowed," admits Mr. Watson, "that outside the range of his hearthstone Surtees, like many a northern squire, was a bit of a tartar. 'I never push myself an inch forwards,' he once confided . . .'but I damned well see I'm never pushed an inch back.'"[80]

In 1837 he ran for Parliament as a Conservative; he dropped out of the race when it became clear to him that he and the Liberal candidate were dividing the votes between them, thus insuring the reelection of the incumbent whom they both wanted deposed. This abortive attempt to run for political office is important because, as a consequence of it, a good deal more can be learned about the character of Robert Smith Surtees. First, there is his own declaration of principles as stated in his address to the electors: "I am a decided friend to Improvement in every shape and way—a Reformer of proved Abuses in Church and State—an Advocate for the fullest Measure of Civil and Religious Liberty that is compatible with the Security of Property and the Maintenance of a National Religion: for Retrenchment and Economy in every Department of the Public Service—for the Extension of Commerce, the Reduction of Taxation, particularly of those that press heavily on the Working Population and for the Diffusion of Useful Knowledge throughout the country."[81] Second, there is the significant respect he earned during the campaign, especially from his opposition. One Liberal newspaper wrote that "the bold and frank demeanour of Mr. Surtees certainly deserved Radical approbation, and made that gentleman an object of respectful treatment." Another described him as "an enlightened and Liberal Tory, whose address is a manly and creditable one, in which he declares his principles without the slightest equivocation." A third confessed that "we were pleased with his spirit and good temper and only regret that he is a Tory."[82]

However one might speculate about the man's character, these words, his own and those of others, show him in the best possible light. True to his usual habit of employing his personal experiences in his novels, he was to reproduce this particular experience in Jorrocks's campaign for Parliament in *Hillingdon Hall* with only one significant difference—Jorrocks wins. Surtees was invited to run for Parliament again in 1838, 1840, 1844, 1847, and 1852, and declined each time; by then his estate, his family, his writing, and his public duties were occupying his time and satisfying his ambition.

There is one more facet of Surtees's character which should be investigated before turning to an analysis of his individual literary works, and that introduces a problem more relevant for the modern reader than it was for people of Surtees's day. It is a question of morality—the morality of hunting, of pursuing a small creature, fox or rabbit, with a pack of trained hounds until the victim drops of exhaustion and is literally torn apart. Many people would not find such sport amusing; they would consider it to be unmitigated cruelty. Probably such a moral stance did not even occur to Surtees, just as it did not occur to Richard Martin, author of the Cruelty to Animals Bill, who, although he did not hunt himself, met the field at Boulogne every afternoon to inquire what sport they had. As Watson points out, "It is important to notice that the *ethical* problem was not conspicuous until the later decades of the Victorian age. The sanctities of animal life troubled people in Surtees's day no more than their fathers had suffered moral embarrassment in trafficking in negro slaves."[83] Surtees himself makes a more relevant analogy in *Plain or Ringlets:* "Tender hearted beauties, who would rush to the rescue of a fly in a cream jug, kept the poor sickly milliner girls sewing all night in order that they might be gay and smart on the morrow."[84] That, to Surtees, was cruelty. As far as hunting was concerned, he defined his values in terms of the hunt itself, the working of the hounds, the skill of the huntsman, the camaraderie of the field, the thrill of the chase—if, after all that, a fox were to die, that occurrence was of no more ethical importance to him than the catching of a fish is to most people today. "Like Smollett and Fielding before him, he approves of hunting as a way of showing the superiority of the fun-loving, energetic, and natural side of human nature."[85] Alex Hamilton explains it this way: "The

coherence of Surtees's fictional world is established by the un-
questioned assumption of every character in it that, while breath
can be drawn, he must somehow keep up the pace. If the reader
cannot see the presence of this human motive as proper to con-
triving the death of a fox, the vitality of Surtees's writing will seem
to him spurious and even offensive. If he accepts it, he has a mount
which will take the obstacles."[86]

All this is not to imply that Surtees had no standards where the
treatment of animals was concerned. Hunting had to be fair: the
game had to have a clean getaway and killing, if there was killing to
be done, had to take place in the open. There was no glory for him
in killing a cornered victim. He fought the increasing trend toward
the use of the bag-fox, animals captured elsewhere and transported
to the hunting field. "Bag fox-hunts, be they ever so good, are but
unsatisfactory things," he writes in *Mr. Sponge's Sporting Tour*.
"The mere retaking of an animal that one has had in hand before is
not calculated to arouse any very pleasurable emotions."[87] Besides,
such a practice was very unfair to the animal, who was forced to flee
for his life through a country with which he was unfamiliar, carrying a strong scent from his captivity that made his destruction inevitable. When Facey Romford is given a bag-fox as a gift by a
woman who knows nothing about the ethics of hunting, he pursues
the fox primarily to see that it gets safely out of the country and
does not fall victim to some stray cur. "Indeed, he kept looking
about in all the unlikely places for a wild fox to be, fearing lest the
unfortunate fugitive should fall into the jaws of the pack without a
chance for his life."[88] The fox "escapes," of course, and Facey, who
shares Surtees's philosophy, merely comments, " 'So much the
better, don't care if he beats us;' adding to himself, 'no credit in
killin' a bag-fox—rather a disgrace, oi should say.' "[89]

Another practice gaining in popularity which Surtees could not
support was hunting the carted deer, a captured deer hauled by its
owner from one rural community to the next for the purpose of
providing amusement to paying participants who were permitted to
chase the desperate animal until it could be cornered and carted up
again. In *Romford* Surtees analyzes "the happy confusion of fiction
with fact" that keeps "the flag of stag-hunting flying in the ascend-
ant."[90] Anyone with romantic visions will inevitably have them
destroyed after one look at poor Benicia Boy cowering terrified in
his cage. "And now, where are all your visions of rousing the
antlered monarch from his lair, ye enthusiastic souls?" he asks. "Or

where the wild expanse of country, ye romantic ones? One view of
the deer-cart on the smooth lawn, has dispelled them all."[91] His dis-
dain for the practice is evident in *Sponge:* "Nobody ever goes fran-
tic at seeing an old donkey of a deer handed back into his carriage
after a canter."[92]

Not even the popular *battue,* the practice of employing scores of
men and dogs to drive all birds and animals within a certain area
from cover in order to kill, with no selectivity or conscience, as
many living creatures as possible, escaped his condemnation; in
Plain or Ringlets he reveals its true nature, slaughter without sport.
The Duke of Tergiversation and nine guests destroy in one after-
noon one hundred pheasants, forty-three hares, six woodcocks,
twenty rabbits, one owl, and a fox. "You exterminate in a day what
should serve you a year,"[93] criticizes the author. Such perversions of
the sport of hunting Surtees could not tolerate, and despite popular
opinion, he attacked them openly, directly, time after time
throughout his novels.

There were other sports besides those associated with hunting
which drew his fire. He strongly criticized any sport which encouraged cruelty, betting, and drunkenness. When he started the
New Sporting Magazine he made his position relative to such sports
clear. "We had expressly stated in our prospectus," he records in his
memoirs, "that Prize-fighting, Bull-baiting and Cock-fighting were
low and demoralizing pursuits and all reference thereto was to be
excluded from our pages."[94] "The fact is," explains Mr. Noakes,
"there was a strong, hard-headed streak of austerity in his character,
and this caused him to be instinctively repelled by the betting element in sports like racing, steeple-chasing, and pugilism."[95] Horse-
racing, for example, he says in *Plain or Ringlets,* encourages "an in-
fusion of gamblers, blacklegs, and pickpockets. . . . Yet races they
have, and announcements are made with great sport anticipated,
and stewards are victimised, and money screwed out of everybody
and from every available source. And for what? . . . In order that
the gamblers may have a field day, and rig the betting lists from
one end of the kingdom to the other." He goes on to reveal how the
races are frequently "fixed." "And that fact alone is enough to
destroy the interest in a race, for as there is no secret so close as that
between a rider and his horse, so though the little gentleman in
black and yellow may work and flourish and appear emulous to win,
there is no saying but his orders may be exactly the reverse, and at

the proper time he will give the gentle pull that enables red and white on the grey to slip in half a head before him."[96] He summarizes his feelings in the words of Lawyer Ballivant's warning to Jasper Goldspink: "As the turf is at present constituted—its vice, its depravities, its atrocities,—I really think a man had almost better be under it than on it."[97] One of Surtees's most famous scenes is that of the "Grand Aristocratic Steeple-Chase" at the end of *Sponge* where he describes not only the selfish aims of the promoters and the benefits to the professional gamblers but the cruel dangers to horses and riders as well. In that catastrophe he has one man killed and several horses gruesomely injured before he finishes with the subject.

"His idea of sportsmanship is perfectly sound," summarizes Mr. W. L. Renwick. "Sport must be free from brutality, an end in itself, with enjoyment as its only reward."[98] It was hunting, without gimmicks, without unwarranted cruelty, without gambling and drunkenness and other social vices, that was the love of Surtees's life. Certainly Jorrocks speaks for his creator when he says, " 'Untin' is the foremost passion of my 'eart! Compared with it all others are flat and unprofitable. It's not never of no manner of use 'umbuggin' about the matter, but there's no sport fit to hold a candle to fox-'untin'. . . . Believe me, my beloved bouys, that 'untin', 'untin', 'untin', is the sport!"[99] And now Surtees found himself in a position where, for the rest of his life, he was free to combine the two foremost passions of *his* heart, his "taste for scribbling" with his enthusiasm for the hunt.

One of Surtees's first actions upon returning to Hamsterley was to start a pack of hounds. "I got hounds,"[100] reads a small slip among the Hamsterley papers. His childhood friend and model, Ralph Lambton, had been paralyzed in a hunting accident, and it is probable that Surtees started his pack, hunting at his own expense, so that sport in the neighborhood could continue. Two years later, in 1840, he gave up the hounds. "The country being very thinly inhabited," he writes, "scarcely any one hunted with me except such friends as happened to be staying with me."[101] Besides, the demands of farming and overseeing tenants, coupled with preparations for his coming marriage, did not leave him time to be a dedicated master of hounds.

On May 10, 1841, Surtees married Miss Elizabeth Jane Fenwick, daughter of Mr. Addison Fenwick of Field House and Pallion Hall.

Aside from the fact that they visited London annually, usually in June or July, and occasionally went on to Paris, very little is known about their domestic life; undoubtedly one could turn to Nimrod's description of Surtees's father's life, apply it to that of the son, and not be far from the actual facts.

Between 1840 and his death in 1864 Surtees held a number of positions of responsibility in the community; the first of these, to which he was appointed in 1842, were Deputy-Lieutenant and Justice of the Peace for Durham County. As was characteristic of Surtees, it did not take him long to use one of those experiences in one of his novels, for in *Hillingdon Hall* Jorrocks, too, is made Justice of the Peace.

There was one duty, however, in which he took no interest, that of major in the Durham militia, the position to which he was appointed in 1844. Since he would brag that "though a major of militia, I never had a sword on,"[102] it is no wonder that an official enquiry was made to him as to whether he would be willing to serve in the event of his unit's being ordered abroad, and he promptly resigned. Mr. Cooper writes that "there seems to have been little chance of the regiment going overseas then or at any other time, and it was probably little more than a courteous enquiry as to whether he proposed to give any attention to his military duties or not. He did not, and his resignation was a sufficient answer."[103] The reason for his indifference to this particular post is obvious when one considers the antimilitary attitudes implied by his satire; he could not see himself as a member of *Young Tom Hall*'s Heavysteed Dragoons. Again one finds obvious parallels between his fiction and his life.

In 1844 he became a member of a committee to devise means of dealing more effectively with Anti - Corn Law League agitation. The Corn Laws taxed import of grain (called "corn" in Britain) in order to protect farmers by helping to keep foreign grain out of Britain; the Anti - Corn Law League consisted primarily of factory owners and workers who were convinced that repeal of the tax would lower the price of bread. Despite the efforts of landowners like Surtees and their supporters in Parliament, anti - Corn Law sentiment grew and, in 1846, following a bad wheat harvest in England which raised the price of bread still higher, the laws were repealed. Surtees immediately turned his attention to a different kind of agricultural reform, the enlarging of grassland and the raising of cattle. When the County Agricultural Protection Society, dedicated to reestablishing an import tax on wheat, invited him to attend one of their meetings, Surtees recognized a lost cause. He answered simply, "Dear Sir,—No more agitation for yours very truly, R. S. Surtees."[104] *Hillingdon Hall*, the novel he was writing at the time of his struggle against repeal, became a vehicle for the direct expression of his political ideals.

During his first years at Hamsterley, between 1836 and 1845, in addition to all his other activities, Surtees completed his first three novels, *Jorrocks' Jaunts and Jollities* (1838), composed of sketches revised from the *New Sporting Magazine*, *Handley Cross* (1843), and *Hillingdon Hall* (1845). With the publication of his third novel he had reached the age of forty and was well settled in his double life of country gentleman and sporting author.

Despite his obligations at home, however, Surtees still enjoyed traveling the country and hunting with various packs of hounds. His situation was considerably different from what it had been as an employed hunting correspondent, for now he could choose the packs he visited and indulge his personal interest in the science of hunting. The winter of 1845 was a particularly good hunting season, and Surtees took that opportunity to publish a series of articles on hunting which appeared from October 1845 to April 1846 in *Bell's Life*. The series was published in book form later in 1846 under the title *Analysis of the Hunting Field*. "In short," he writes in the preface, "the volume is written with a view to upholding the great national sport of hunting in its purest, most legitimate form, and of decrying all attempts at money-making out of what ought to be sheer pleasure."[105]

The *Analysis* is interesting for more than its descriptions of hunting, though, for here Surtees was writing essentially humorous nonfiction, presenting his real, personal views on those same subjects which he satirized in his novels and presenting personal experience in a way that proves much of his fiction is not exaggerated. For example, there is his discussion of hunt dinners, a favorite literary subject. "Hunting and hospitality are almost synonymous," he informs his reader, "and the man who hunts a country must calculate on a good deal of knife-and-fork work. Dining out much is hard work—dreadful where a man is 'cock' guest every time. Still a Master must undergo it." He goes on to describe the typical dining room, "which would accommodate eight comfortably, or ten in a pinch, is now made to hold eighteen. Of course the curtains are all drawn, the shutters are shut, and there is a rousing fire." The

dinner progresses. "Seventeen glasses of wine at dinner! Awful! Awful at any time, but doubly so when supplied by a bumper-filling
clown, who will shut out the skylight, or give the objector the
balance over his hand or up his sleeve"(5 - 7). The book is brim-
ming with good advice. "Have a good fire in each guest's bedroom
when they arrive," the author suggests. "People out of gigs, off
coaches, out of railway trains are apt to be chilly and cold" (8). He
even provides marital counseling. "While nibbling our pen, we
have been casting about to see if we could collect any instance,
among our numerous acquaintance, of a bad foxhunter husband,
and we are happy to say we have drawn a blank. . . . Indeed, if we
were a young lady, we would pick a foxhunter for preference" (14).
Sometimes he waxes philosophical. "It is indiscriminate *cold-
blooded drinking* that should be avoided. It is a dangerous, a
ruinous thing. One glass this year leads to two next, and so they go
on till ruin is the result" (75). It is not surprising that the *Analysis*
has been considered by later critics and historians to be "a valuable
social document."[106]

Besides the publication of his *Analysis of the Hunting Field* and
his two novels, *Hawbuck Grange* (1847) and *Mr. Sponge's Sporting
Tour* (which appeared first in serial form from January 1849 to April
1851 and was not published in one volume until 1853), there was
another happy occurrence in the life of Surtees during this time, the
birth, in 1847, of his only son, whom he named Anthony, as all first
sons of that branch of the family were named. Two daughters,
Elizabeth Anne and Eleanor, were born later.

For the rest of his life Surtees spent the majority of his time at
Hamsterley, engaged in official duties, enjoying his family, super-
vising his estate, hunting, and writing. *Sponge* enjoyed great popular success, and Surtees, at the age of forty-seven, after twenty-
three years of writing, had finally "arrived." In 1854 *Handley Cross*
was republished, complete with illustrations by John Leech, and by
1858 the author could say of it, "I believe it was paying something,
at all events it was out of debt last summer."[107] He continued to
serve his county in whatever way he could; in 1852 he became
Chairman of the Shotley Bridge Bench (and solved a crisis arising
from roaming mad dogs) and in 1856 he was appointed High Sheriff
of Durham County (and immediately reduced the circuit judge's
entourage from a carriage and four to a carriage and two).

In 1861 he wrote an analysis of the problems of local farmers, his
"Description of Durham," much of which restates ideas he also

presented in his novel *Ask Mamma*. It also contains high praise for his friend and neighbor Mr. Ralph Lambton.

There was another project which Surtees undertook for which he has received insufficient credit—he conceived the idea for the *Field* and served in its early years as a kind of editor-in-reserve as well as chief correspondent for its first issues. "I would make it a sporting, a farming, a landowner's, and a sort of high-life-in-London paper—with a summary of all that is going on," he suggested. "There is an undoubted field for a gentleman's sporting paper, and by eschewing politics, of which we all have *quantum suff* in the dailies, you will embrace readers of all opinions and offend none."[108] It is interesting that his original suggestion for the paper's title was the *Nimrod* and that it was changed only on the insistence of the publishers. To fill the pages of the early editions Surtees undertook in 1852 another hunting tour. When asked to serve as editor of the hunting department for the new journal, however, he turned down the position. "At this distance from the Press I fear the damage arising from sporting misprints will more than counterbalance any benefit from my communications," he wrote, obviously showing a distaste for the idea of moving back to London. "Any hunting man on the spot could do it in an hour, but I can't do it by intuition on the Border."[109]

In 1856 he also volunteered to edit a new edition of Blaine's *Encyclopaedia of Rural Sports* which ran to 1,230 closely printed pages with 600 illustrations, quite an undertaking in itself.

In addition to all this he published three more novels, *Young Tom Hall* (part of which ran in the *New Monthly Magazine* from October 1851 through January 1853 but was never completed), *Ask Mamma* (1858), and *Plain or Ringlets* (1860), and completed a fourth, *Mr. Romford's Hounds*, which was to be published posthumously in 1864.

When the weather was bad for hunting and the winter lessened the duties of the farmer, Surtees often left Hamsterley to seek a warmer climate. It was his custom on those occasions to travel with his wife to Brighton, the scene of so many fond memories and the place that inspired Handley Cross and Roseberry Rocks. The winter of 1864 was especially severe, with the frost lasting well into March, and the couple left home to spend a few days in London, after which they traveled on to Mutton's Hotel in Brighton. There, during the night of March 16, Surtees awoke with pain in the region of his heart. Ten minutes later he was dead. His death was unexpected; at the age of fifty-eight he still enjoyed good health and still hunted regularly.

What is especially revealing about the man's character is that, despite his own advances toward fame and fortune, he had never lessened his efforts to help people who needed his aid: one of his last confrontations was in behalf of an aged cottager named Athey who had lost his Poor Law Relief for keeping two cows. Surtees managed not only to restore the relief, but also to uncover the fact that the Poor Law Guardians were taking pay for their services, a scandal which he immediately reported to their superiors. He was always concerned about the poorer classes and wrote a letter to the *Times* of London to protest the conditions existing in workhouses. To rectify the situation somewhat he became guardian of the parish of Meadomsley and urged his friends to do likewise in their own areas "to the end that the boards, having on them men with a sense of responsibility and endued with ordinary conceptions of humanity, might remedy the many defects and short-comings."[110] Perhaps Surtees chose not to be a crusader in his fiction, but a more active, concerned humanitarian in his personal life would be hard to find. Mr. Boville, in his *England of Nimrod and Surtees*, assures his readers that "he was much respected in his own countryside for a kind and generous heart and a great sense of public duty."[111]

By 1864 Surtees had finished writing *Mr. Romford's Hounds* and was waiting for Leech to find time in his busy schedule to do the illustrations before publishing it. "It will be the last serial I shall attempt,"[112] he wrote to Leech, for he had turned his attention to another project, the writing of his memoirs, which he intended to entitle *Sporting and Social Recollections*. Unfortunately, after his death his sketchy notes for the book were accidentally filed away with papers he had written in connection with his duties as Justice of the Peace. They were not uncovered until many years later, when they were edited by Mr. E. D. Cuming and published in 1924 as *Robert Smith Surtees, Creator of "Jorrocks" by Himself and E. D. Cuming*. Another significant note found among those Hamsterley papers indicated that *Recollections* was to be published under his own name, a break with the anonymity of over thirty years' standing.

It is said of Thackeray that once, on picking up the biography of an author, he remarked, "I hope there will be none of this damned nonsense about me when I am dead." . . . It is easy to imagine Surtees, who was Thackeray's friend, saying the same thing, for they had many tastes in common and not least a hatred of display and habit of decent reticence. Nor, it must be admitted, was it a life so abounding in incident or romance as to attract the biographer in search of a story: still less was it touched with scandal so as to attract the biographer in search of sensation. It is the story of a country gentleman and sportsman, more erudite and articulate than most of his fellows: devoted to his family and his estate, serious and knowledgeable about his sport: austere in private life but no Puritan: a loyal and generous friend, a resolute but not implacable enemy: honest and courteous, conscious of his own importance and ready to defend it, but never to assert it: prudent in money matters, hating extravagance and empty show. Apart from his writing, it is a life such as thousands of country gentlemen have lived.[113]

CHAPTER 2

The Jorrocks Trilogy

I Jorrocks' Jaunts and Jollities

T HE Jorrocks stories that appeared in the *New Sporting*[1] were intended to serve two purposes: first, to describe for members of London's new "Cockney" mercantile middle class those places available to them which they may or may not have discovered; and second, to supply information on the sporting scene for regular readers of the magazine. Consequently, Jorrocks can be found indulging in sports in localities within easy reach of London, such as Margate and Herne Bay, or venturing farther away to Cheltenham and Brighton, or even, on one terribly daring occasion, traveling all the way to Paris. Along the way, between his adventures and misadventures, Jorrocks manages detailed, witty, and usually outrageously prejudiced descriptions of the places he visits and the people and activities he encounters. In these sketches John Jorrocks, eccentric, amusing, and ill-fated as he is, is not, for the most part, the *raison d'être* for the stories; rather, he is a kind of literary shield behind which Surtees can duck while tossing critical darts at the world. Jorrocks is so opinionated, and his words and actions frequently so absurd, that no one is likely to take him seriously. Consequently, Surtees, the man who, after all, provides Jorrocks with those biased opinions, is able, by using Jorrocks as his mouthpiece, to say anything he likes about his fellow citizens, their cities and their pursuits, without anyone's taking offense. So successful is his craftsmanship that the reader forgets, just as he is supposed to do, that the book has an author at all.

Perhaps it was his own love of the country that led Surtees to be particularly critical of the cities and towns he describes, or perhaps he was diplomatically appealing to his readers' prejudices, the countrymen for the country and the Londoners for London, but in any event no place he describes fares well. For example, when Jorrocks travels to Newmarket for the horse races in "The Turf: Mr. Jorrocks at Newmarket," he looks with "a sort of sleepy astonishment at the smallness of the place, inquiring if they were sure they had not stopped at some village by mistake." Surtees goes on to assure his readers that "wiser men than Mr. Jorrocks have been similarly disappointed, for it enters into the philosophy of few to conceive the fame and grandeur of Newmarket compressed into the limits of the petty, outlandish, Icelandish place that bears the name." He takes his criticism further, giving his readers what is obviously intended as a kind of travel-guide warning: "We know of no place where a man, not fond of racing, is so completely out of his element as at Newmarket, for with the exception of a little 'elbow shaking' in the evening, there is literally and truly nothing else to do."[2] Jorrocks's first impressions of Herne Bay in "The Day After the Feast" are equally unflattering. " 'My eye,' said Jorrocks . . . 'wot a pier, and wot a bit of a place, why, there don't seem to be fifty houses altogether, reckoning the windmill in the centre as one' " (217). In "Aquatics: Mr. Jorrocks at Margate," while Jorrocks walks the streets of that popular vacation spot Surtees comments on both the city and the eccentricities of the people who flock there. "How strange that man should leave the quiet scenes of nature, to mix in myriads of those they profess to quit cities to avoid! One turn to the shore, and the gas-lights of the town drew back the party like moths to the streets, which were literally swarming with the population. 'Cheapside at three o'clock in the after-noon,' as Mr. Jorrocks observed, was never fuller than Margate that evening" (109).

The inhabitants of these towns receive no better treatment. When Jorrocks tries to strike up a conversation with people on the streets of Newmarket he is met with nothing but abuse.

"Pray sir," addressing himself to a groomish-looking man . . . "pray sir, be this your principal street?" The man eyed him with a mixed look of incredulity and contempt. At length, putting his thumbs into the armholes of his waistcoat, he replied, "I bet a crown you know as well as I do." "Done," said Mr. Jorrocks, holding out his hand. "No—I won't do that," replied the man, "but I'll tell you what I'll do with you,—I'll lay you two to one, in fives or fifties if you like, that you knew before you axed, and that Thunderbolt don't win the Riddlesworth." "Really," said Mr. Jorrocks, "I'm not a betting man." "Then, wot the 'ell business have you at Newmarket?" was all the answer he got.

Two more rebuffs of this sort send Jorrocks back to his room "not in the best possible humor" and lead Surtees to comment on "the extreme sharpness and suspicion of the people" of Newmarket (78). Here is one example where Jorrocks serves directly as spokesman for his creator, for Surtees, in his memoirs, mentions that Nimrod, in search of information about racing, went to Newmarket, "notoriously the worst place possible; for at Newmarket they can't even tell you what o'clock it is without offering to couple the hour with some other event."[3]

And in this vein Jorrocks continues to warn readers of other cities of Surtees's acquaintance. When arriving in Boulogne, warns the author in "The Road: English and French," the visitor must "take his chance among the touts and commissionnaires of the various hotels who are enough to pull passengers to pieces in their solicitations for custom" (136). Surtees's description of the reception which new arrivals could expect when disembarking at Margate is one of the most powerful of the lot, and could well have discouraged anyone who read it from undergoing the ordeal.

Two or three other cargoes of cockneys having arrived before, the whole place was in commotion, and the beach swarmed with spectators as anxious to watch this last disembarkation as they had been to see the first. . . . Those who stand on the beach, outside the rails, are just on a right level to shoot their impudence cleverly into the ears of the new-comers, who are paraded along two lines of gaping, quizzing, laughing, joking, jeering citizens, who fire volleys of wit and satire upon them as they pass. "There's *lee*tle Jemmy Green again!" exclaimed a nursery-maid with two fat, ruddy children in her arms, "he's a beauty without paint!" "Holloa, Jorrocks, my hearty! lend us your hand," cried a brother member of the Surrey Hunt. Then there was a pointing of fingers and cries of "That's Jorrocks! that's Green!" "That's Green! that's Jorrocks!" and a murmuring titter, and exclamations of "There's Simpkins! how pretty he is!" "But there's Wiggins, who's much nicer." "My eye, what a cauliflower hat Mrs. Thompson's got!" "What a buck young Snooks is!" "What gummy legs that girl in green has!" "Miss Trotter's bustle's on crooked!" from the young ladies of Miss Trimmer's seminary, who were drawn up to show the numerical strength of the academy and act the part of walking advertisements (107).

It would take a strong stomach and invincible ego to survive such scrutiny; no doubt Surtees saw himself, with these and similar warnings, as doing his readers an invaluable service.

The *New Sporting* was, however, chiefly concerned with sport, and almost all the Jorrocks stories deal with some kind of sporting event. Horse-racing is the subject of two stories, "The Turf: Mr.

Jorrocks at Newmarket," and "Sporting in France." When
Jorrocks's friend the Yorkshireman Mr. Stubbs first suggests going
to Newmarket, Jorrocks's reaction is exactly that of Surtees. "Oh!
Newmarket's a dreadful place, the werry name's a sickener" (72).
He does go though, and that evening "no sooner was Mr. Jorrocks
left alone with his candle, than all at once he was seized with a
sudden fit of trepidation, on thinking that he should have been in-
veigled to such a place as Newmarket" (76). Surtees's descriptions
of the races themselves and the activities which surround them are
classic in their color, their attention to detail, and their ability to
transport the reader directly to the scene. They show the amazing
power of this young apprentice writer.

The majority of the ring rush to the white judge's box, and have just time to
range themselves along the rude stakes and ropes that guard the run-in,
and the course-keeper in a shooting-jacket on a rough pony to crack his
whip, and cry to half a dozen stable lads to "clear the course," before the
horses come flying towards home. Now all is tremor; hope and fear
vacillating in each breast. Silence stands breathless with expectation—all
eyes are riveted—the horses come within descrying distance—"beautiful!"
three close together, two behind. "Clear the course! clear the course! *pray*
clear the course!" "Polly Hopkins! Polly Hopkins!" roar a hundred voices
as they near; "O, Fy! O, Fy!"respond an equal number. "The horse! The
horse!" bellow a hundred more, as though their yells would aid his speed,
as Polly Hopkins, O, Fy! and Talleyrand rush neck-and-neck along the
cords and pass the judge's box. A cry of "dead Heat!" is heard. The
bystanders see as suits their books, and immediately rush to the judge's box,
betting, bellowing, roaring, and yelling the whole way (83).

If Surtees had his doubts about Newmarket, at least there he found
the races exciting. In Paris, he warns his readers, they had better be
prepared for a totally different scene.

Mr. Jorrocks, indeed, indifferent as he is to the affairs of the turf, could not
suppress his "conwiction" of the difference between the flibberty-gibberty
appearance of the Frenchmen, and the quiet, easy, close-sitting jockeys of
Newmarket. . . . Then such riding! A hulking Norman with his knees up
to his chin, and a long lean half-starved-looking Frenchman set astride like
a pair of tongs . . . followed by a runaway English stable lad . . . and half
a dozen others equally singular, spurring and tearing round, throwing
gravel and sand into each other's faces, until the field was so separated as to
render it difficult to say which was leading and which was
trailing. . . . Then what an absence of interest and enthusiasm on the part

of the spectators! Three-fourths of them did not know where the horses started, scarcely a man knew their names, and the few tenpenny bets that were made, were sported upon the colour of the jackets. A Frenchman has no notion of racing (171,173).

Descriptions such as these leave no doubt about the young Surtees's natural writing ability; his "taste for scribbling" was most certainly matched with a great deal of natural talent. His readers were indeed fortunate to receive such practical information in so entertaining a manner.

Most of the stories, as one would expect, deal with some form of hunting. In "Surrey Shooting: Mr. Jorrocks in Trouble," Jorrocks hunts "Old Tom,—a most unfortunate old hare" (47) and is arrested for trespassing by the length of his big toe (and is found guilty). He visits a stag-hunt in "Mr. Jorrocks and the Surrey Staghounds" where the carted deer, "a lubberly-looking animal, as big as a donkey, blobbed out, and began feeding very composedly" (64). The stag escapes temporarily by jumping into the open door of a vacant carriage passing along the road, and the hunters have to pay her fare in order to retrieve her and continue the hunt.

But it is fox-hunting that claims his heart. "Fox-'unting is indeed the prince of sports. The image of war without its guilt and only half its danger. I confess that I'm a martyr to it—a perfect wictim—no one knows wot I suffer for my ardour—If ever I'm wisited with the last infirmity of noble minds, it will be caused by my ungovernable passion for the chase. The *sight* of a *saddle* makes me sweat. An 'ound makes me perfectly wild. A red coat throws me into a scarlet fever"(71 - 72). It is in these stories that Surtees first argues the value of the subscription pack and the dedication and skill of the Cockney hunter. The Surrey pack in "The Swell and the Surrey" and "The Yorkshireman and the Surrey" has two runs as long, exciting, and skillfully handled as the most sophisticated hunter could dream of. While it is true that one of these ends with the hounds devouring a rabbit that a neighboring farmer has just shot instead of the fox they were supposedly tracking, it must be remembered that it was the chase that interested Surtees, not the kill. The ending here is not intended to show Cockney sportsmen in a bad light, but rather to add one more to the long list of Jorrocks's personal catastrophes.

One particular trait of the author is well illustrated by these two stories—his inclination to have a bit of fun even with those things and those people he admired. "The members of the Surrey are the people that combine business with pleasure," he writes in "The Swell and the Surrey," "and even in the severest run can find time for sweet discourse, and talk about the price of stocks and stockings. 'Yooi, wind him there, good dog; yooi, wind him.'—'Cottens is fell.'—'Hark to Cottager! Hark!'—'Take your bill at three months, or give you three and a half discount for cash' " (10). The first time countryman Surtees encountered such talk on the hunting field it must have sounded peculiar indeed. But he waited to see how such strange conversationalists would conduct themselves, and he found more about them to praise than to laugh at. "One of the most striking features in the aspect of this chosen region of fox-hunting," he declares, "is the quiet, easy manner in which the sportsmen take the thing. . . . There is no pushing, jostling, rushing, cramming, or riding over one another; no jealousy, discord, or daring; no ridiculous foolhardy feats; but each man cranes and rides, rides and cranes, in a style that would gladden the eyes of a director of an Insurance office" (10). Occasionally this tendency of his to mix humor with seriousness, to satirize what he respects, to laugh at one aspect of a thing while praising the whole, makes it difficult for the reader to define just what Surtees *is* implying, just how he *does* feel about a particular subject. But such confusion is usually short-lived, for when one finishes reading a story or novel by Surtees he finds that not only has he acquired an understanding of the values of the author, but also that those values have somehow become his own. The fact that he often does not know exactly when or how his own attitudes have been so manipulated is the highest tribute that can be paid to the subtlety and skill of the writer. This, then, is the nature of the "travel agency" and "sporting-information" services provided by these stories, and, as they appeared in the *New Sporting*, these were their main functions.

When the stories are placed together, however, as they are in *Jorrocks*, and considered as parts of a single literary work, they take on considerably more significance. For one thing, they introduce and begin the development of the character of Jorrocks. Although the Jorrocks of these stories is the kind of comic antihero that has a good deal of public appeal, he is not, when one considers *Jorrocks* as a whole, a particularly well-developed character. His main function in every story, besides that of serving as Surtees's spokesman, seems to be to come to some ludicrous end. When he swims at Margate he loses his pantaloons to the incoming tide. When he travels to Paris he falls victim to the supposed Countess Benvolio who, in Jorrocks's words, "certain*lie* is a bad 'un" (183), making her living from men she attracts on the road between Boulogne and Paris by inviting them to stay with her and then, when their money has all been spent to her advantage, handing them a bill for their room and board. When he fishes at Herne Bay he upsets the boat and almost drowns, but the seriousness of even this potentially tragic situation is undercut by his dream that "Neptune has appointed me huntsman to his pack of haddocks. Have two dolphins for my own riding, and a young lobster to look after them. Lord Farebrother whips in to me—he rides a turtle" (228). When he hunts with the Surrey pack he is tossed into an "unsavoury cesspool," coming out "completely japanned with black odoriferous mixture" (37). When he boards a boat he gets seasick, and when he rides a carrousel in France he becomes dizzy and falls "to the ground like a sack. . . . He had fallen on his head, broken his feather, crushed his chapeau bras, lost off his mustachios, was as pale as death, and very sick" (179).

Even in his own home, as in "Mr. Jorrocks' Dinner-Party," he is not immune to mishap, for when he gives a dinner he is first among those present to become completely intoxicated, although he carries the incident off in true and endearing Jorrocks fashion: "His legs deserted his body, and, after two or three lurches, down he went with a tremendous thump under the table. He called first for 'Bat-say,' then for 'Binjimin,' and, game to the last, blurted out, 'Lift me up!—tie me in my chair!—fill my glass!' " (212).

All these misfortunes, when spread over a period of several years as they were in the *New Sporting*, probably seemed amusing to the magazine's readers, but when they are all put together in one volume as they are in *Jorrocks*, they become so predictable that they take their place in the ranks of the most blatant "formula" fiction. Surtees was still experimenting with his subject, as Mr. Watson points out. "John Jorrocks proceeded to maturity by easy stages. As the London sportsman and Coram Street grocer his introductory and haphazard appearances were no more than promising. At his worst, as in Paris or at Newmarket, he was frankly a bore; in matters of law he was, and remained, a reluctant medium for Surtees' memories of the courts. Jorrocks made, in short, several trial trips, and invariably—or almost invariably—returned to dry dock for overhauling."[4]

And yet, in spite of this redundancy and unevenness observable to the distant critical eye, the reader of *Jorrocks* is never for one minute bored by the stories. Each one is told with such attention to detail that it is an immediate and fresh experience. People are described by the expressions on their faces, the cut of their clothes, the nuances of their conversations, and, consequently, every character, no matter how minor, is an individual. Every carriage, every dining room, every round of boiled beef and plum pudding is different from every other one. With such realism as this to surround them, even the improbable adventures of John Jorrocks seem almost plausible.

Jorrocks' Jaunts and Jollities serves not only as an introduction to Jorrocks, but also as an indication of the direction which Surtees's humor and satire were to take in later writings. Already one can see Surtees setting up his duality between his good, honest men and his artificial hypocrites, for one of Jorrocks's greatest attributes is his absolute naturalness; he does and says whatever he feels like doing and saying, seldom weighing the consequences and never worrying about his image or his popularity. There is absolutely no phoniness about him, and, because of that, he attracts people to him in spite of his outspoken and often controversial ideas. "He does not pretend to be anything but what he is," Surtees himself wrote about Jorrocks in his preface to the second edition of *Jorrocks*. "He plays his part without affectation, which is what we wish other people would do."[5] On just one occasion does Jorrocks allow himself to be seduced into affecting the "swell"—the Countess Benvolio manages to get him into the dress of a "nondescript-looking militaire with fierce mustachios" and a "large sword" (152). He enjoys the role for a time but, because his natural Jorrocksian self *will* show through, he can not carry it off with the aplomb of the consistently artificial dandy. Attending a Paris ball, for instance, he "was seen poking his way through the crowd with a number of straws sticking to his feet. . . . The fact was, that Agamemnon had cleaned his shoes with liquid varnish (French polish) and forgetting to dry it properly, the carrying away half the straw from the bottom of the fiacre was the consequence" (160). When "in an unlucky moment he took it into his head he could waltz," the inevitable result is a terrific collision with another couple, "ending by all four coming down upon the hard boards with a tremendous crash" (161).

The reader does not like Jorrocks in this disguise, for he knows, and Jorrocks does not, to what extent the hero is being lowered to the level of the scheming countess and her artificial Parisian society. Surtees emphasizes the point when Jorrocks fails to recognize the true quality and character of those attending the grand ball. "The ball proceeded with the utmost decorum, for though composed of shopkeepers and such like, there was nothing in their dress or manner to indicate anything but the best possible breeding. Jorrocks, indeed, fancied himself in the very elite of French society" (160). He is finally undeceived when M. Eugene, with whom he has had the unfortunate tumble on the dance floor, challenges him to a duel; Jorrocks appears at the appointed time and place—the boasting, threatening Frenchman does not. Two days later when he returns to the countess's apartment to find a German burgomaster comfortably installed in *his* easy chair, before *his* fire, with *his* mistress, Jorrocks suddenly sees the whole truth. Poor Jorrocks, "shocked at the duplicity of the Countess, the umpudence of Rosembom, and the emptiness of his own pockets, bolted away without saying a word" (182). Jorrocks has had his initiation into the artificiality and hypocrisy of society—and the reader has had his initiation into this important element of Surtees's satire.

The stories furnish many more examples of Surtees's favorite caricature, the humbug. There is, of course, the "Swell," popularly identified as Nimrod, whose true self is revealed in "The Swell and the Surrey" on that great social leveler, the hunting field. He is last seen "inwardly promising himself for the future most studiously to avoid the renowned county of Surrey . . . religiously resolving, at the same time, to return as speedily as possible to his dear Leicestershire; there to amble o'er the turf, and fancy himself an 'angel on horseback' " (21). Nosey Browne in "Surrey Shooting" is another kind of "swell," a Londoner whose "affairs having gone crooked . . . was taking his diversion on his wife's property" (41). It is about him that Surtees makes his well-known statement that "there is nothing a cockney delights in more than aping a country gentleman" (45). He is to show many, many examples of such absurdity (Marmaduke Muleygrubs of *Handley Cross* and Sir Moses Mainchance of *Ask Mamma* are obvious examples); as a true "country gentleman" himself he could not stand to see that dignified position degraded by fools. Unfortunately Jorrocks himself in *Hillingdon Hall* becomes just such a character, and it ruins the novel.

Others of Surtees's favorite satirical targets come in for their first ribbing here. In "A Week at Cheltenham," for example, doctors are accused of being "rum Jockeys" who "say one word for the patient and two for themselves" (90). Lawyers are shown in a bad light, for when Jorrocks appears in court in "Surrey Shooting," "Mr. Smirk . . . having deliberately unfolded his brief, which his clerk has scored plentifully in the margin, to make the attorney believe he had read it very attentively, rose to address the Court—a signal for half the magistrates to pull their newspapers out of their pockets, and the other half to settle themselves for a nap" (49 - 50).

Arranging for Jorrocks to meet and befriend a French baron in "The Turf" provides Surtees with an opportunity to indulge his personal prejudice by making fun of foreigners; it is the least successful type of humor attempted in the Jorrocks stories, and fortunately Surtees did not try it again until his introduction of Prince Pirouetteza in *Plain or Ringlets* twenty years later. The use of foreign dialect did give Surtees an excuse to exercise a more challenging form of humor, however—verbal humor, extremely popular in the sporting literature of the day. The book is filled with puns, many distressingly stilted, a few genuinely clever. For example, when Jorrocks accompanies the baron to buy a horse, the Frenchman asks about the horse "vot ears he has?" The trainer first responds, "They show breeding," and then, upon repetition of the question, "Well, but he carries them well." Someone finally figures out that the baron is asking the horse's age. A few minutes later he states, "I vill my vet" and is offered glasses of water and of brandy before he manages to stutter, "I vill von *wet-tin-nin-na-ary* surgeon" (79). When the hunted stag starts down a country road, "a Kentish waggon drawn by six oxen, taking up the whole of the lane, had obliged the *dear* animal to take to the fields again" (65—emphasis by Surtees). When Jorrocks goes to court his lawyer argues "that a grosser attack was never made upon the character of any grocer" (50). The other lawyer explains the law of trespass by pointing out that "if any part of the toe was there, the law considers that it was there in *to-to*" (55—emphasis again by Surtees). Still stinging from his rough treatment at the hands of his French countess, in "Sporting in France" Jorrocks meets Nimrod, who asks about Paris, "What pleased you most—the Tuileries, Louvre, Garden of Plants, Pere la Chaise, Notre Dame, or what?" Jorrocks replies, "Why now, to tell you the truth, singular as it may seem, I saw nothing but the Tuileries and Naughty Dame—I saw a wery naughty dame, for she fleeced me uncommonly" (183). Fortunately the young Surtees either tired of this particular brand of humor, popular though it was among his contemporaries, or discovered that, taken to such absurd lengths, it had no place in more mature fiction.

II   Handley Cross

"The reader will have the kindness to bear in mind, that the work merely professes to be a tale, and does not aspire to the dignity of a novel."[6] So states Surtees in his preface to *Handley Cross*. A reader on first approaching the book may feel an inclination to doubt the author's word (the 1926 edition runs to 578 pages), but when one comes to summarize the plot, the wisdom of that analysis becomes clear—as far as a story line is concerned, almost nothing happens. Yet the book is full of adventures, of tension and conflict, of funny people doing funny things and not-so-funny people doing petty and selfish and cruel things. In spite of the novel's lack of traditional dominating "plot," it is one of the most engrossing books written and the most popular of Surtees's novels. The very nature of its free and easy style, so much like life itself as lived from day to day with no great "climax" or obvious "denouement" or other literary artifice, gives the book its charm.

The story centers around the adventures of John Jorrocks during the year he serves as Master of Fox-Hounds to the Handley Cross pack. Before that occasion Mr. Jorrocks was considered "a great city grocer. . . . As a merchant he stood high—country traders took his teas without tasting, and his bills were as good as bank notes. Though an unlettered man he had great powers of thought and expression in his peculiar way. He was 'highly respectable,' as they say on 'Change—that is to say, he was very rich, the result of prudence and economy" (56).

Handley Cross is one of the numerous health spas built on mineral springs which had been very exclusive and relatively insignificant until the advent of the railroad, after which time "the Handley Cross mania spread throughout the land! Invalids in every stage of disease and suffering were attracted. . . . The village assumed the aspect of a town. . . . Buildings shot up in all directions. Streets branched out, and markets, and lawns, and terraces stretched to the right and the left, the north, the south, the east, and the west" (15). As the town increases the number of its tourist attractions, the population expands accordingly, its ranks swelled primarily by London's new "Cockney" middle class: young men coming for adventure and old men to escape the drudgery of their shops, rich men to waste their money and poor men to make their fortunes, mothers to marry off plain daughters and pretty girls to attract husbands; and, in the end, everyone comes to Handley Cross because everyone else is there. This is the scene Jorrocks enters, a lively playground populated by every imaginable character type.

The leading citizens of Handley Cross have long been aware of the benefits which a good fox-hunting establishment would bring their community, and when they offer the positon of master of hounds to Jorrocks he is beside himself with joy. " 'My vig!' exclaimed Mr. Jorrocks, jumping from his chair, slapping his thigh, and hopping round the table. . . . 'My vig! who would have ever thought of such a thing!—O, John Jorrocks! John Jorrocks! you are indeed a most fortunate man! a most lucky dog!' " (60 - 61).

Jorrocks is a cautious man, however, and a good businessman. He knows that as master of hounds he will be responsible for hiring and supporting a professional huntsman as well as supplying and feeding the hounds and a number of horses, and since his only remuneration will be the income from subscriptions, the operation will have to be large enough and good enough to attract a sizable number of sportsmen. Therefore the condition of the establishment he is about to inherit is of utmost importance to him. In his reply to Captain Miserrimus Doleful, the town's master of ceremonies, he first assures him that "I am a sportsman all over, and to the backbone.—'Unting is all that's worth living for—all time is lost wot is not spent in 'unting—it is like the hair we breathe—if we have it not we die—it's the sport of kings, the image of war without its guilt, and only five-and-ten per cent of its danger" (64). He is completely sincere here; just as in *Jorrocks' Jaunts and Jollities* he is absolutely obsessed with hunting. He does not allow his enthusiasm to master his good sense, however.

I have no manner of doubt at all, that I'm fully qualified for the mastership of the 'Andley Cross fox-hounds, or any other. . . . But enough of the rhapsodies, let us come to the melodies—the £ s.d. in fact. Wot will it cost? . . . how many *paying* subscribers have you? Wot is the *nett* amount of their subscriptions—how many couple of 'ounds have you? Are they steady? Are they musical? How many days a week do you want your country 'unted? Is stoppin' expensive? What 'un a country is it to ride over? . . . Are your covers wide of the kennel? Where is your kennel? . . . wot stablin' have you? Is 'ay and corn costly? . . . Write me fully—fairly—freely—frankly, in fact, and believe me to remain, gentlemen, all your's to serve (64).

Not only does poor Doleful not know the answers to half these questions, but he is afraid to answer the other half for fear of losing Jorrocks. Suddenly he hits upon a brilliant subterfuge. "A rival has appeared for the mastership of the hounds," he tells Jorrocks, "and an influential party is desirous of getting the hounds for him" (67). All too clearly the grocer sees the dream of a lifetime slipping away, and in desperation he accepts the Handley Cross hounds, sight unseen.

Upon his arrival in Handley Cross he is given a hero's welcome—bands play, children march, people line the streets—all carefully arranged by Captain Doleful. From the balcony of the Dragon Hotel he addresses the cheering throng. "You see I've come down to 'unt your country, to be master of your 'ounds, in fact. . . . In short, I means to be an M.F.H. in reality, and not in name" (87 - 88).

As he soon realizes, Jorrocks could not possibly have made a promise more difficult to fulfill, and the rest of the novel details his adventures as he tries to transform the sorry remnants of the Handley Cross pack into a respectable hunting establishment. He trains the hounds to hunt fox rather than chickens, sheep, and Handley Cross citizens. He hires James Pigg as huntsman, a colorful "character" from "Cannynewcassel" with a dialect so thick no one can understand him but Jorrocks and the hounds. He buys and sells horses in various deals ranging from the ridiculous to the sublime. He enlarges his territory, taking his hounds to such places as Cockolorum Hall, the home of Mr. Marmaduke Muleygrubs, and the Pinch-Me-Near Forest. He gives sporting "lectors," presides at hunt banquets, and falls off his horse numerous times. He gets lost, and robbed, and laughed at by the great sporting author Pomponius Ego. And through it all, he eats and drinks, drinks and eats, and hunts, hunts, hunts.

All this is great fun for Jorrocks and the reader, and it is too bad the novel does not end with one more last hunting day or with Jorrocks hiccuping through one last toast. For the ending of *Handley Cross* is decidedly unsatisfactory. Two trials constitute what could be considered the climax of the novel. Both occur after the hunting season is over and Jorrocks has returned to London; once the hero leaves the scene of the action the reader is expecting the book to come to a swift conclusion and is not prepared for a humorous novel to become suddenly and unexpectedly tragic. The first trial does little to alter the tone of the novel or the reader's ex-

pectations. Doleful, after a long negotiation by letter with Jorrocks
in London, buys one of Jorrocks's horses. "Like most young horse-
masters, Captain Doleful did not give his new purchase much
rest. . . . This, with indifferent grooming and very indifferent
keep, soon reduced the once sleek and pampered hunter to a very
gaunt, miserable-looking dog-horse. . . . The horse grew daily
worse, and a cough settled upon him that seemed likely to finish
him. . . . The Captain was thrown on his wits for getting out of
the purchase." First he tries subtlety: "I thought he looked queer
when I bought him . . . and it is well the loss falls on one so well
able to bear it as the wealthy Mr. Jorrocks." Jorrocks ignores this
hint and several others, and Doleful at last resorts to threats. "I now
demand a return of the money I paid for your nasty diseased horse,
which an honest English jury will award me in the event of a
refusal." Jorrocks responds in astonishment, "I doesn't know
nothin' wot an honest English jury may do for you, but this I knows,
I'll do nothin'. Zounds, man! you must be mad—mad as a hatter!
Let's have no more nonsense" (449, 452). Doleful chooses to continue the "nonsense," however, and decides to drag his former
friend into court. Surtees uses this trial scene primarily for one purpose, to satirize legal practices and practitioners much as he had
done in the similar trial scene in *Jorrocks' Jaunts and Jollities*. In
tone it is perfectly consistent with the rest of the novel up to that
point. He introduces "superintendents Shark and Chizeller, both
pompously drunk" (473). He speaks of "the gentlemen of the jury,
many of whom are deaf" (481). The jury is finally sent out to
deliberate "in some safe place, without meat, drink, or
fire. . . . Twelve strangers are thus left to make each other's acquaintance by arriving at the same conclusion" (491). The jury
decides in favor of Jorrocks. There is nothing in this trial scene, in
the unintelligible testimony of Pigg, in the self-interest of the
witnesses, not even in the lawyers' obvious manipulation of the
facts, that foreshadows the tragedy of the trial to come.

"Scarce were the rejoicings for his victory over Doleful finished,
ere our worthy friend found himself involved in a more delicate and
difficult dilemma than he had ever yet known . . . we may briefly
state, that our worthy friend's jollities or eccentricities at length
earned him a commission of lunacy." Apparently the publicity
which the Doleful trial receives in the London papers brings
Jorrocks to the attention of "his next-of-kin, with whom our worthy
friend had long been on indifferent terms, or rather no terms at all."

For the first time they realize that he is a master of hounds. "To the uninitiated, the idea of keeping a pack of hounds is looked upon as the surest proof of riches or ruin; an opinion that is periodically confirmed by the papers, in announcements of the great expense certain establishments are kept up at. . . . The expense of Mr. Jorrocks' hounds was estimated in like ratio" (496 - 97). What the trial amounts to is an attempt by Jorrocks's relatives to have him proven insane so that they can get their hands on his money. But as far as Surtees is concerned, the real defendant is not Jorrocks, but fox-hunting. Mr. Moonface, lawyer for the plaintiff, characterizes the hunting scene as "noisy, boisterous, clamorous—*riotous*" and describes the "unhallowed scenes of riot and confusion, days made horrible with yelling, and nights spent amid the wildest, the most unprofitable debauchery" which were held in "open defiance of the statute against 'riots, routs, or unlawful assemblies' " (500 - 502). Now the reader knows these charges to be untrue, just as he knows Jorrocks to be perfectly sane. He has followed Mr. Jorrocks through numerous hunts; he has learned the art of hunting and experienced the thrill of the chase and the elation of victory; he has laughed at Jorrocks and pitied him and worried about him and come to know and admire him. But the significant point is that none of the jurors has had the same experiences. None of them is familiar with hunting; they are all city men ranging in occupation from "Feather and Court Head Dress Maker" to "Dustman." They allow themselves to be taken in, not by evidence, but rather by their own prejudices. Because hunting is unfamiliar to them they allow themselves to be persuaded that it is a "mad and unnatural pursuit" (500), and because Jorrocks participates in it, he, too, must be "mad and unnatural." "We ask you," the lawyer pleads, "to save this unfortunate gentleman from himself, and from the consequences of his own acts" (505). The appeal to emotion is absurd—Jorrocks, of all men, is perfectly capable of taking care of himself.

The trial fills three chapters. All the evidence against Jorrocks seems adequately refuted. Jorrocks and Pigg interrupt the proceedings with humorous protestations and comments. Satire of the court and its methods continues, a bit less blatantly, perhaps, but nevertheless in the same manner as that of the former trial. Now that Surtees has had his fun at the expense of the judicial system, revealing, just as he did in the last trial scene, the lawyers' manipulating the evidence and playing on the emotions of the jurors as well as the willingness of the uneducated jurors to be persuaded by emotional rhetoric, the reader is prepared for another declaration of innocence. Only by reading the novel himself can one understand the reader's shock, disappointment, and indignation when the jury returns with a verdict of " 'Insanity,' adding that 'Mr. Jorrocks had been incapable of managing his affairs since he took the Handley Cross Hounds' " (529).

Surtees had clearly made his point about the absurdity and unfairness of the legal system. He had answered all ridiculous arguments against fox-hunting. "What induced Surtees to jeopardize *Handley Cross* with this incredible episode?"[7] asks Mr. Watson. Susan Hallgarth has a theory which provides at least a possible explanation. "The 'madness' of Jorrocks," she claims, "like the madness of Quixote before him, is a measure of the madness of the society around him—as Jorrocks calls it, 'the werry age of balderdash and 'umbug—balderdash the grossest, and 'umbug the greatest that . . . the intellect can . . . conceive.' "[8]

In a world where common sense and natural exuberance have the appearance of madness, Jorrocks and his kind are aberrant; and in a world where dishonesty and artificiality are the rule, he has no place. Hence with the Insanity Hearing, Surtees transposes his satire to a somewhat larger theme—the insufficiency and "madness" of the middle-class ethic which was changing his world. Significantly, the jury is composed of London merchants who are totally ignorant of hunting and whose notion of virtue is limited to the Victorian ideals of temperance and industry. For such men, hunting is not only incompatible with their "idea of a rational life" but an occupation at odds with "the steady course of mercantile life." As the defendant, Jorrocks represents the old life of humor and good fellowship—the world of hunting in which the summit of ambition is the position of M.F.H. . . . Like Falstaff and Don Quixote before him, Jorrocks is one of those mad fools whose wisdom goes begging in the everyday world.[9]

Perhaps Surtees did have this point in mind, but if so, then his satire is more complex, his thinking, if not more profound, at least on a much broader scope than at any time in any of his other novels. Certainly he attacked the values of society, but in every other instance he did so in one of two ways, either by caricaturing specific individuals who represent the foibles of society as a whole, or by stepping outside his stories and, assuming the role of familiar narrator, addressing his audience directly. If he did indeed intend to make such a serious critical point here, then he failed to communicate it effectively simply because the reader is too emotionally

involved with Jorrocks at that moment, too stunned by his momen-
tous defeat, to take such a long-distance critical view. It is obvious
that Surtees is equating the attack on hunting with the attack on
Jorrocks; in this he is perfectly consistent, for he almost always
measures people, in one way or another, against that universal test
of character, and in this case the test reveals the jury's fatal flaw.
But if he meant more than that, if he was indeed trying to make the
point Ms. Hallgarth articulates so well, then he failed and never
tried such a tactic again. If he was not trying to make such a point,
then he was guilty of bad literary judgment, a charge that can very
seldom be leveled against him.

Unfortunately, the outcome of the trial virtually destroys the rest
of the novel. Even Surtees seems at this point to have lost interest,
for after a couple futile attempts at humor he ends the book quickly
and completely predictably. Doleful's inheritance of a small fortune
from a lady admirer is clumsily handled, and Mrs. Jorrocks's
machinations to get her niece Belinda married to Doleful are merely
pathetic. Even the potentially humorous scene where Doleful is
tricked into buying a wig and false beard is undermined by the
reader's awareness of Jorrocks's situation. By the time Doleful is
finally captured by the fortune-hunting Miss Brantingham the
reader is totally indifferent and merely wants the book to end. The
author does, of course, eventually rectify Jorrocks's condition, for
just before the novel closes Jorrocks regains his freedom after a contrived scene in which he is interviewed by the chancellor, who finds
him "an enthusiast" but sane (559). With no more ceremony than
that, Jorrocks is released, too late to regain the reader's enthusiasm,
too late to clarify any grand social significance, and too late to save
the ending of *Handley Cross*.

One point must be made here, not in defense of the book's conclusion, which is the most unsatisfactory that occurs in any of
Surtees's novels, but perhaps as a partial explanation for it. *Handley
Cross*, like most of his books, appeared first in magazine installments, this one in the *New Sporting Magazine*. During the time
of its initial publication Surtees was occupied with his marriage, his
hounds, and the duties incumbent upon him as new owner of
Hamsterley. As a result the installments did not appear regularly
and the story was composed of just twenty chapters. If this revised
edition is disappointing, imagine the dismay of Jorrocks's fans
reading the original version, which ended with the trial for lunacy
and the advertisement of "a first-rate pack of fox-dogs, twenty-five

couple in all, to be sold." When the story was scheduled to appear
in its three-volume edition Surtees did extensive revising, some, no
doubt, on the suggestion of John Leech, the book's illustrator, who
agreed that "your notion of introducing fresh matter is, I think, excellent," and went on to recommend that "while you are about it I
think I would get old Jorrocks into a good deal more fun before
making him a victim."[10] This Surtees did; he included, for instance,
Jorrocks's invitation to Nimrod and the "sporting lectors" which
had appeared earlier as separate papers in the *New Sporting*. And,
in recognition of the wholly unacceptable ending, he added the extra chapters to the end, thus leaving Jorrocks a free man, Belinda
happily married to Stobbs, and Doleful recovering from the shock
of his marital mistake. It is obvious patchwork and, unfortunately,
all the patches show.

But weak though the ending may be, it does not detract from the
delight of the rest of the book. *Handley Cross* is not a novel of action so much as it is a novel of character, and it is filled with
strange, eccentric, peculiar people that make one think immediately
of Dickens. Dominating them all, of course, is John Jorrocks.

"Prune down a little of the coarseness of the fox-hunting grocer,"[11] suggested William Sholbert, literary adviser to Surtees's
publisher, Colburn. It seems strange to readers of today that
Jorrocks should once have been considered particularly "coarse,"
especially in *Handley Cross* (although that adjective does come
close to describing him as he is presented in *Hillingdon Hall*) for
now critics place him "with Falstaff and Sir Toby Belch, Mr.
Pickwick and Mr. Micawber, in the gallery of the great comic
characters in English Literature."[12] Leonard Cooper identifies the
qualities shared by such successful comic figures, and, as he points
out, all of their attributes can be applied directly to Jorrocks.

The truly great comic character is rare—much more rare than the hero or
the tragic figure. He is rare because he is the most difficult person of all to
create. Unless he is to deteriorate into a butt, a mere figure of fun, he must
be, as Falstaff was, "not only witty in himself but a cause of wit in
others"—a cause of wit, be it noted, not a target for it . He must possess a
definite character of his own with attributes which are lovable and even admirable and he must be to a certain extent in control of events and not entirely at their mercy. He may love food and wine, but not be a glutton or a
drunkard, suffer mischances, but never be quite overcome by them, indulge his fancy and his wit but never lose touch with reality. He must in
fact, unless he is to degenerate into the pure buffoon, have the natural

dignity which comes from being a genuine and complete person. Above all he must be aware of his own weaknesses, able to laugh at them, but on occasion able to conquer them. And perhaps even most important he must be ready of speech, quick at repartee and easily quotable. Given these qualities—and it is a formidable list—he may do almost anything, because he will be able to extract humor from anything.[13]

Jorrocks's "boisterous enthusiasm places him squarely in the tradition of stock British braggarts who stemmed from characters like Ralph Roister Doister, acquired excess weight and humours during the Renaissance (Jonson's Bobadil, Chapman's Quintilliano, and of course, Falstaff), and finally fused with the picaresque idealism of Don Quixote in the eighteenth and nineteenth centuries (in Sterne's Uncle Toby, Smollett's Matthew Bramble and Commodore Trunnion, and Dickens's Mr. Pickwick),"[14] adds Susan Hallgarth in her discussion of Jorrocks's place in literary history. In addition to fulfilling the above criteria, the character of Jorrocks is successful for three additional reasons: first, his personality is comprised of those human qualities which all honest readers must recognize, sometimes to their embarrassment or amused chagrin, in themselves; second, he is somehow able to transcend those same human frailties in a way which leaves the reader amused and sometimes envious; and third, he is a complete, unique personality who will remain in the reader's memory, to be chuckled at and wondered over, for the rest of his life.

Surtees's development of just one such human trait can be used to illustrate the complexity of Jorrocks which so surprises and delights the reader, as well as the author's sound intuitive understanding of psychology necessary to make Jorrocks a man with whom the reader will identify. Self-assurance, for example, is one of Jorrocks's sterling qualities, as that off-hand comment to Doleful, "I have no manner of doubt at all, that I'm fully qualified for the mastership of the 'Andley Cross fox-hounds, or any other" clearly illustrates. Because of his confidence in his own abilities he expects the rest of the world to be immediately conscious of his merit and to treat him accordingly. When he is invited to Pluckwelle Park to look at a horse owned by Sir Archibald Depecarde, a man whom he has never met, Jorrocks casually responds, ". . . as the M.F.H. 'ears it is a goodish distance from Handley Cross, he will bring his night cap with him, for where the M.F.H. dines he sleeps, and where the M.F.H. sleeps he breakfasts" (121). What reader does not wish he had the courage to respond in a similar way to those who make unreasonable demands?

Even more enviable is Jorrocks's ability to bluff his way out of awkward situations. One afternoon the hunt is overtaken by a storm and Jorrocks, separated from the hounds, is thoroughly drenched, bitterly cold, and hopelessly lost when he stumbles up to the gates of Ongar Castle. At first, when he is greeted with great cordiality and shown to a room with a roaring fire, a hot bath, and fresh evening clothes laid out on the bed, he assumes that Pigg has arrived before him and warned of his coming; when he realizes that such is not the case, however, he takes the strangeness of the situation completely in stride—after all, he is John Jorrocks, Master of Fox-Hounds, and such treatment is his just due. He is, of course, a victim of mistaken identity, the servant having assumed that he was one of the gentlemen invited there. Poor Jorrocks, sitting in his bath and sipping more brandy than is helpful to clear thinking, is actually shocked to hear another man at the door demanding entrance. "I will thank you, sir, " insists the voice, "to let *my* servant remove *my* clothes from *my* room." "My good friend," replies Jorrocks, " 'ow is it possible for me to part with the garments when I've nothin'o'my own but wot's as drippin' wet as though I'd been dragged through the basin of the Paddin'ton Canal?" The man on the other side of the door becomes increasingly more impatient. "*Will you open the door, I say?*" " 'No I von't,' replied Mr. Jorrocks, 'and that's the plain English of it!' So saying, he swaggered back to the fire with the air of a man resisting an imposition. He then mixed himself a third tumbler of brandy and water" (194).

The reader's emotions as he encounters this scene range from mystification (*he* doesn't take that reception and those clothes for granted) to shock (Jorrocks's actions *are* outrageous) to a sense of victory when that bizarre behavior results in an invitation to dinner and a night's lodging. Most readers imagining themselves in a similarly awkward situation know that they would become apologetic and self-conscious and desire nothing so much as to disappear completely. They would be haunted by discomfort for days. But not Jorrocks! Certainly his self-confidence occasionally borders on pomposity, but wouldn't most people rather be that way than extremely meek or self-deprecating? Of course his courage is sometimes, as it is in this case, fired by drink, but the reader knows Jorrocks can drink a great deal and in this scene is far from drunk. He is simply a man whose self-esteem will not allow him to be pushed around, and almost any person would like to be able to say the same about himself. Although the reader realizes intellectually that Jorrocks's actions and attitude here are not really admirable, nevertheless most readers could not help but feel just a bit of respect for the man.

Self-assurance is not Jorrocks's only or even his predominant characteristic, however; it is just one facet of his entire personality. He is a big man and strongly prefers not to have to jump fences in pursuit of the fox ("I never goes off the 'ard road if I can 'elp it," he confesses—314). He rides miles out of his way to find a gate, looking over his shoulder all the time to make sure no one notices and inventing a plausible excuse in case anyone does. But he is not a complete coward; he will jump when necessary, as the number of his journal entries for "catchin' my 'oss" and "stoppin' my 'oss" indicate (274). In spite of his confidence he can recognize when he is in a nasty predicament and his lamentations on those occasions are enough to make even the hardest-hearted reader feel pangs of pity. One day when the hunt leaves him behind he feels very sorry for himself indeed.

Oh dear! oh, dear! wot shall I do? wot shall I do—gone away at this hour—strange country—nobody to pull the 'edges down for me or catch my 'os if I gets spilt, and there's that Pigg ridin' as if there was not never no such man as his master. Pretty kettle of fish! . . . Oh dear! oh dear!, was there ever sich a misfortinate indiwidual as John Jorrocks? . . . Oh dear! oh, dear! I wish I was well back at the Cross, with my 'ounds safe i' kennel.—Vot a go is this!—Dinner at five—baked haddocks, prime piece of fore chine, Portingal honions, and fried plum-puddin'; and now, by these darkenin' clouds, it must be near four, and here I be's, miles and miles away (186 - 187).

Jorrocks also flirts outrageously, even going so far as to arrange an assignation with Sir Archey Depecarde's maid. He drinks too much and thinks about food almost as much as he does about hunting. He is proud of his origins, admitting freely that his mother was a washerwoman, and never once feels ashamed of being a merchant among gentry or a Cockney among squires. He hates pretension and artifice. He is an excellent master of hounds, proud of his position, knowledgeable of his duties, and fond of horses, hounds, and humans alike. He is prudent and practical without being stingy. He is open and trusting with people, so much so that some of them, his servant Benjamin, for example, take advantage of him. He is also willing to speak out for justice and to defend those he believes in. "Who's made my Pigg so drunk?" he demands one morning when he arrives late to the scene of the hunt and finds that the field have been buying his huntsman drinks. "Didn't leave his sty so. . . . Well, gen'l'men, I 'opes you're satisfied wi' your day's sport!—you've made my nasty Pigg as drunk as David's sow, so now you may all go 'ome" (280). Altogether he is full of cheerfulness and enthusiasm and honesty and a zest for life that makes him, John Jorrocks, an unforgettable experience.

The pages of *Handley Cross* are replete with a seemingly endless variety of "characters"; many of them are included for some obvious satiric purpose, but that fact does not, by any means, spoil their individual charm. Perhaps one reason for their originality lies in Surtees's lifelong habit of observing people, noticing in detail their features, their dress, their eccentricities, and reproducing those people, sometimes wholly and sometimes in combination, upon the pages of his books. His society was certainly not devoid of models, as Mr. Watson points out.

The period 1800 - 40 was not only remarkable in appetites and clothes, but also in "characters" and in the production of those eccentricities whose fast-vanishing survivors were still a pleasant, if accidental, encounter even as late as the nineties. Esmé Wingfield-Stratford has commented with truth, "The Victorian was pre-eminently an age of characters in fiction. May we not be permitted to conjecture that this was because it was an age of characters in life?" . . . Both in England and Scotland every locality possessed, in pre-railroad days, its "characters," those originals who handled life in a spirit of comedy or tragedy, but never of mediocrity. . . . They were the children of small communities, with home education or no education, liberty from the conventions, and encouraged by the delighted plaudits of their environment.[15]

Surtees's notes for his memoirs are filled with descriptions of the eccentrics he knew personally such as the Jack Johnson who, with his wife, operated the "outdoor confectionary department" at Ovingham, selling the boys "inferior gingerbread, and what would now be thought most repulsive-looking sweets." "It was Jack's pleasure to keep a cuddy," Surtees writes, "and, not liking to buy fodder, he used absolutely to go about the lanes in summer clipping grass for hay with a pair of scissors."[16] There was also Brooke Richmond, "the hero of Boulogne," who "practiced eccentricity with great effect." "His forte," reports the author, "was drawling through his nose, and walking, or rather lounging, about the town in a woolly white hat, dressed otherwise as a common sailor, led like a blind man by a white bulldog." And then there was the strange

case of Jerry, the race list seller from Newcastle, who always wore
"a cocked hat with feather" and sometimes "an old admiral's coat."
But "Jerry had this peculiarity, which does not always attend full-
dress attire—namely, that when he wore his cocked hat and feather
he generally went bare-foot." In addition "He had a quizzing glass
made of the neck of a bottle suspended by a blue ribbon, with
which he used to reconnoitre his acquaintance and ogle the fair."
"Some said Jerry feigned madness," writes Surtees, "but I think it
was real."[17] Although neither Johnson nor Richmond nor Jerry ever
found his way into any of Surtees's novels, at least not in
recognizable form, such people were evidently in abundance. In
other words, Surtees's characters must have seemed to readers of his
own day more familiar and less like caricatures than they seem to
readers today.

For example, there is one of his classic characters, James Pigg,
Jorrocks's huntsman, a "dry-tongued, uncouth, hard-riding
northerner"[18] whose character is based on that of a Durham
blacksmith and sportsman named Josh Kirk, who for a time served
as huntsman and whom Surtees undoubtedly met on the hunting
field. Many of Pigg's expressions and even some of his adventures
come directly from Mr. Kirk. Mr. Watson in his 1933 book on
Surtees verifies that "the exterior of Kirk was, according to Mr.
Scarth Dixon (who is surely in this year of grace the last man to
have hunted with Surtees), an exact replica"[19] of Pigg, who is introduced to the reader in anything but complimentary terms. "He
was a tall, spindle-shanked man, inclining to bald, with flowing
grey-streaken locks shading a sharp-featured, weather-beaten face,
lit up with bright hazel eyes. A drop hung at his nose, and tobacco
juice simmered down the deeply indented furrows of his chin"
(148). One of Pigg's most ingenious schemes, whether it originated
with him or Mr. Kirk, is turning himself into "a sort of Insurance
Company" which "issued tickets against hunting accidents—similar
to what railways companies issue against railway ones. By these he
undertook for a shilling a day or five shillings the season, to insure
gentlemen against all the perils and dangers of the chase—broken
necks, broken backs, broken limbs, broken heads, and even their
horses against broken knees" (176). Precisely because he is based on
a real person and thus presented "without sentimentality . . . in all
the crudity of nature and not as an idealized figure,"[20] is Pigg a truly original literary character. "When it comes to James Pigg,"
Moira O'Neill points out, "comparisons fail. The man from Canny

Newcassel is unique. His simplicity and his shrewdness, his honesty and his lying, his obstinacy, his intrepid courage, his taste for 'brandy and 'baccy,' and his over-mastering passion for hunting—none of these qualities are so very exceptional in themselves; yet their combination in Pigg is a masterpiece of originality. Jorrocks himself is less remarkable than Pigg . He sometimes reminds us of other fat men in other fields of literature, and very fat men are always declining towards farce. But Pigg reminds us on no one, and he is in the purest vein of comedy."[21]

And there is, of course, the representation of Nimrod as Pomponius Ego that drew the critics' fire. Jorrocks invites the sporting correspondent to Handley Cross because, as he confesses in his letter, *"entre nous*, as we say in France, I want to be famous, and you know how to do it." Describing Ego to Pigg, Jorrocks warns that "if by any unlucky chance he blames an 'untsman, or condemns a pack, it's all dickey with them for ever; for no livin' man dare contradict him, and every one swears by wot he says. . . . I question if the world would not have been as 'appy without the mighty Hego." "Oh, Pigg," he mourns in justified trepidation, "hambition is a frightful, a dreadful thing!" (367 - 369). When Ego finally arrives and Pigg fails to recognize him, Ego's scorn is absolute. " 'Humph!' said Ego to himself, 'a rummish genius this, I guess—I am POM-PO-NIUS EGO,' observed he, with an air of annihilation." He does not fare much better with Jorrocks, who compliments him after a joke with "Haw! haw! haw! werry good joke, Mr. Hego, werry good joke, indeed—have laughed at it *werry* often" (374 - 375). Needless to say, Ego has his revenge, for in his article he describes in detail how Jorrocks fell off his horse and deliberately refers to Pigg by "the appropriate name of Hogg" (390). In a very lengthy report he summarizes the entire day's hunt, including an excellent run, by saying, "After a good deal of cold and slow hunting, we at last worked up to our fox, and Mr. Jorrocks most politely presented me with the brush, in terms too flattering and complimentary to admit of my repeating it here"(392). Needless to say, far from flattering Mr. Ego, Jorrocks had inadvertently criticized the author while praising his own hounds. "Am sorry you weren't hup to see the darlin's run into the warmint," was what he really said. "Did it in style! Never were sich a pack as mine; best 'ounds in England!—best 'ounds in Europe!—best 'ounds in Europe, Hasia, Hafrica, or 'Merica!" (387). "This sort of hoiling won't answer," moans Jorrocks. "Always one word for his host and two for himself." No wonder Surtees named this character Pomponius Ego, and no wonder Nimrod took offense! After reading the account, poor Jorrocks now knows firsthand those evils of "hambition,"and, for the only time in his life, he *"couldn't eat a bit"* (394).

There are dozens of other characters and character types who come in for their satirical blows in this novel, all of them representatives of Surtees's world of unnatural phonies whose hypocrisy and affectation reveal themselves in contrast to the real, natural Jorrocks. There is, for instance, the pseudo-doctor who helped to establish the fame of Handley Cross, "a roystering, red-faced, round-about apothecary," with "every requisite for a great experimental (qy. quack) practitioner,—assurance, a wife and large family, and scarcely anything to keep them on" (912 - 913). There are the lawyers Shark, Chizeller, Lollington, Screecher, Prettyman, and Badlad, whose very names characterize their performances. There is the pretentious Mr. Marmaduke Muleygrubs, who had been a stay-maker in London until he inherited a large fortune from an uncle. "On getting this he cut the shop, bought Cockolorum Hall, and having been a rampant Radical in the Ciry, was rewarded with a J.P.-ship in the country." Muleygrubs parades Jorrocks past an impressive gallery of fake ancestors (" 'Such a lot of stay-makers!' as Mr. Jorrocks observed"), serves him a terrible dinner despite the huge array of silver plate on the table (" 'God bless us! what a dinner!' ejaculated Mr. Jorrocks, involuntarily"), and subjects the Handley Cross hounds to a hopeless day of hunting for, as his small daughter confides, "P-a-a-r shoots the fox" (308 - 334). The contrast between Jorrocks's honesty and Muleygrubs's hypocrisy is very striking indeed. A great range of humanity is presented in this novel, from a crazy man who rants and raves and jumps on the table to a kind farmer who befriends James Pigg. There are dozens of sportsmen and innkeepers, servants and squires, coachmen and dandies, every one cleverly drawn, and every one different from every other. For what Surtees did in this novel was to place Jorrocks in a position where he comes into contact with two elements of society, the sporting world to which he limits himself in *Jorrocks*, and the world of nonsporting country society to which he limits himself in *Hillingdon Hall*. In *Handley Cross* the entire panorama of human nature is, for one reason or another, attracted to the resort area and, as a result, is passed before the reader, making the book invaluable for those who enjoy sitting in their armchairs watching the parade of humanity go by.

When one looks beneath the surface of the novel, however, it becomes apparent that Surtees is presenting a great deal more than the humorous adventures of a collection of strange characters. His opinions concerning the inadequacy of the legal system and the quackery of the medical profession are clearly communicated. His hatred of hypocrisy and sham, his respect for individuality and personal strength and dignity, are also obvious. Considering his background, Surtees was a surprisingly democratic man. His elevation of the grocer and tea-dealer John Jorrocks to the esteemed position of Master of Fox-Hounds made clear to the world his belief in a man's being judged on his individual abilities rather than either the old or the new social criteria, his family connections or his fortune. "Here was the Cockney sportsman immortalized once and for all. It was comic, it was outrageous, but, what was really important, it was also prophetic. The genius of the Cockney in his exuberance, his self-assurance, his shrewd and deliberate estimation of his own blunt capacity—this genius, now so familiar but then quite revolutionary, was grasped by Surtees, and made immortal in John Jorrocks."[22]

Finally, *Handley Cross* is one of fox-hunting's greatest memorials. No one can read the novel without wishing himself there. Just one short run with the " 'Andley Cross 'ounds" serves to illustrate the fast paced excitement that abounds.

The pack have now got together, and all are busy on the scent . . . . "Dash my vig, he's been here," says Mr. Jorrocks, eyeing some feathers sticking in a bush. . . . The hounds strike forward, and getting upon a grassy ride, carry the scent with a good head for some quarter of a mile, to the ecstatic delight of Mr. Jorrocks, who bumps along, listening to their music, and hoping it might never cease.

A check! They've overrun the scent. "*Hie Back!*" cries Mr. Jorrocks, turning his horse round; "gone to the low crags I'll be bund—that's the way he always goes; I'll pop up 'ill, and stare him out o' countenance, if he takes his old line;" saying which, Mr. Jorrocks stuck spurs into Arterxerxes, and, amid the grunts of the horse and the rumbling of the loose stones, succeeded in gaining the rising ground, while the hounds worked along the brook below. The chorus grows louder! The rocky dell resounds the cry a hundred fold! The tawny owl, scared from his ivied crag, faces the sun in a Bacchanalian sort of flight; wood-pigeons wing their timid way, the magpie is on high, and the jay's grating screech adds wildness to the scene. What a crash! Warm in the woody dell, half-circled by the winding brook . . . the old customer had curled himself up to sleep till evening's dusk invited him back to the hen-roost. That outburst of melody proclaims that he is un-

kennelled before the pack! . . . There, as Mr. Jorrocks sat, with anxious
eyes and ears, devouring the rich melody, he sees what, at first sight, looked
like a hare coming up at a stealthy, stopping, listening sort of pace; but a
second glance shows that it is a fox. . . . The hounds gain upon him, and
there is nothing left but a bold venture up the middle, so, taking the bed of
the brook, he endeavours to baffle his followers by the water. Now they
splash after him, the echoing banks and yew-studded cliffs resounding to
their cry. The dell narrows towards the west, and Mr. Jorrocks rides forward
to view him away. . . . Pigg's horn on one side, and Jorrocks's on the
other, get the hounds out in a crack; . . . and the three sportsmen are as
near mad as anything can possibly be. It's ding, dong, hey away pop with
them all!
     The fallows carry a little, but there's a rare scent, and for two miles of ill-
enclosed land Reynard is scarcely a field before the hounds. Now Pigg
views him! Now Jorrocks! Now Charley! Now Pigg again! Thirty couple of
hounds lengthen as they go. . . . The fox falls back at a wall, and the
hounds are in the same field. He tries again—now he's over! The hounds
follow, and dash forward, but the fox has turned short up the inside of the
wall, and gains a momentary respite. Now they are on him again! They
view him through the gateway beyond: he rolls as he goes! Another moment, and they pull him down in the middle of a large grass field! (422 -
424)

     Nowhere has a sport been presented more attractively or with
greater accuracy. A testimonial to the continued popularity of
Surtees's descriptions of the hunt is the existence of a slim volume
entitled *Hunting Scenes from Surtees*, published in 1953, which is
composed solely of such scenes. Mr. Watson reminds the reader
"that the greatest comic novel on fox-hunting is also the greatest
text-book, and that the finest lecture on the subject ever delivered is
given, not when Jorrocks is off the scene, but by the Cockney
M.F.H. himself."[23] It is, states Aubrey Noakes, "essentially a noisy,
vital book. . . . The over-whelming impression with which we are
left after laying *Handley Cross* down is of its tremendous zest and
'swing.' "[24] One could certainly do worse things with his leisure
time than spend it with Surtees and *Handley Cross*. And for those
who have already spent leisure time with *Handley Cross*, W. C.
Rivers reminds them that it is one of "the two best books to re-read
that I know."[25]

III   Hillingdon Hall

Critics have an interesting tendency to apologize for Surtees's

third novel. "*Hillingdon Hall* may not be a thriller," writes
Frederick Watson. "If it is dull, it is at least knowledgeable."[26] Sa-
soon prefers to pretend the book doesn't exist. "We cannot believe
that [Jorrocks] retired to Hillingdon Hall. . . . For us he is still
trotting out to a bye-day at Pinch-me-near Forest."[27] Mr. Rivers is
even more direct. "*Hillingdon Hall* is, alas! the most unsuccessful
sequel ever penned. The little finger of *Handley Cross* is thicker
than the loins of *Hillingdon Hall.*"[28] The critic for the *Times* of London who calls it "a slough of dullness,"[29] however, goes too far;
there is no question but that it is inferior to *Jorrocks' Jaunts and
Jollities* and especially to *Handley Cross*, but for the reader who is
not familiar with the earlier novels and has, therefore, no basis for
comparison, *Hillingdon Hall* would provide a good-humored
glimpse into one segment of Victorian life, that of the gentleman
farmer.

Jorrocks is once more the center of attention; in this novel he has
left his thriving London business in the hands of his subordinates
and moved his family to the estate of Hillingdon Hall, where he
"means to take a hundred or a hundred and fifty acres in hand, and
try all the new experiments on a liberal scale—guano, nitrate o'
soder, bone manure, hashes and manure mixed, soot, salt, sand,
everything in fact; shall lector on agricultur, and correspond with
the Royal Society, and so on."[30] His talk is more impressive than his
achievements, however, for his knowledge of the subject of
agriculture is limited to what he has read in books, and, besides, he
is not overly ambitious and farming takes more work than he is willing to invest. For the sake of appearances he "rode about surveying
his estate, looking at pigs and cows and sheep, asking foolish
questions, and talking a great deal of nonsense about farming.
Thanks, however, to the veneration in which townspeople, above all
Londoners, are held in the country, the rustics thought some new
lights must be breaking in the husbandry horizon—never imagining
for a moment that the owner of so fine an estate, with such a fine
open countenance of his own, knew nothing whatever of what he
was talking about"(38). His greatest accomplishment as a farmer is
winning first prize with his white bull at a local fair—a bull that had
just recently been given to him by his new acquaintances the Duke
of Donkeyton and the Marquis of Bray. Despite the fact that he
constantly confuses two agricultural products, the pine tree and
pineapple, he does gain a certain amount of local fame based
primarily on two inventions, the first a draining tile composed of
clay, gravel, lime, and coarse brown or Muscovado sugar (146), and

the second an inspiration by Surtees, a "steam-happaratus or hengine that will do at one 'go' wot now takes I doesn't know how many 'ands, and how many 'osses, or how many hours to accomplish," a "monster reaper" that also ploughs the land "so that reapin' and sowin' go 'and in 'and" (155 - 156). As his expectations for it grows, the machine becomes "my grand reaper, plougher, sower, thresher, grinder, &c." (236). Unfortunately, the machine never gets beyond the dreaming stage. Although he might not know a great deal about the practical aspects of farming himself, Jorrocks, like Surtees, knows where to put his faith. "Oh, but science is the ticket; neat genuine unadulterated science. Everything now should be done by science. The world's on the wing, and why shouldn't farmers take flight?" (156 - 157).

Jorrocks does a bit of social and political flying himself before the novel ends. He rather forces his attentions on the Duke of Donkeyton who makes the mistake of inviting Jorrocks, along with dozens of other guests, to a dinner party held solely to promote the duke's political influence. "Mr. Jorrocks was staggered, and Mrs. Jorrocks dumbfounded. They thought it must be a hoax. The idea of them whose most aristocratic acquaintance was Old Lady Jingle, at Margate, jumping all at once over the heads of baronets, baron lords, earls, and marquises, and arriving by one flying leap at a dukedom, was altogether incredible" (58). The success of that dinner can be measured by the vehemence with which the duke receives the suggestion of inviting Jorrocks to his castle a second time. " 'Can't stand him! can't stand him!' exclaimed the Duke, shaking his head again; 'far too hospitable for me, far too hospitable for me—no getting him away from the table—no getting him away from the table . . . should be very glad to see him to dine—monstrous glad to see him to dine—only he is such a man for his bottle—such a man for toasts—such a man for speeches—such a man for drinking things three times over—gives me a headache to think of it,' added his Grace, pressing his hand on his forehead"(232).

Evidently the duke finds it easier to promote Jorrocks than to dine with him, for when an opening occurs he offers Jorrocks the commission of Justice of the Peace. Jorrocks accepts, of course, reminding the duke that "I need not inform your Grace of all the greatness that belongs to the grand order of beak; how they sit with their hats on, how they order people out o' court, and how they return thanks for their healths at farmers' dinners, and expound the

grand duties and dignities of beaks" (187). After such a great distinction ("a regular clothes-basketful of honour"—185), he has to
remind himself, "Vell, for all this I am but mortal man" (202). Unfortunately he is as uninitiated in the duties of magistrate as he is in
those of farmer, first examining the bumps on the culprits' heads to
determine their character ("bampology as he called it"—207) and
then frequently turning them over to his maid Betsey for flogging
with the order, "Give him a good basternaderin'—good strappin',
that's to say . . . and put a pair o' stockins in his mouth, so that we
mayn't be troubled with his noise" (214).

The novel closes with the high-point in Jorrocks's career, his election to Parliament. The circumstances leading to his election are
quite complex (based in part on Surtees's own experiences as candidate for that office). The Marquis of Bray is the natural choice for
the district, but wishing to assure himself all the votes, his position
statement is carefully worded to say absolutely nothing, thus not
committing him to any stand on any issue. While that strategy
might have worked in the past, it proves completely ineffective in a
country raging over the question of whether or not to repeal the
Corn Laws. The Anti - Corn Law League sends a representative to
oppose Bray; Bray's lawyer, Smoothington, manages to buy off the
opposition with a considerable sum of money and assurances that
the marquis is also opposed to the Corn Law. Before he leaves,
however, the discouraged candidate papers the town with banners,
placards, and handbills proclaiming "Great Fact! The Duke of
Donkeyton a Total Repealer!" (471). The farmers are outraged;
they turn to Jorrocks with a plea that he represent their interests by
running against Bray. Jorrocks assents, somewhat reluctantly, and
no one is more surprised than he at his final two-vote victory.
Jorrocks's election reflects not only Surtees's personal experience in
the political arena but also his sensitivity to the entire political
scene. His purpose behind Jorrocks's election, suggests Ms.
Hallgarth, is to demonstrate that "since politics . . . is a matter of
practical, common-sense experience, an untrained Cockney who has
lived and worked in the world may be better suited for parliament
than his 'blooded' opponents."[31] It is Aubrey Noakes who reminds
the reader of still another important point, that "Surtees was one of
the first novelists to detect and write about the pressure-group in
politics when it was still a quite novel thing."[32]

One of the great disappointments in this novel, especially for
those familiar with the earlier two, is the character of Jorrocks.

Away from the hunting field where he had a great amount of expertise and removed from the other eccentric characters of Handley
Cross with whom his own oddities blended almost to the point of in-
visibility, he becomes here a rather tiresome boor. Whereas in
Handley Cross the reader identified with him sufficiently to make
him always a sympathetic character, in this book the reader remains
painfully aware that Jorrocks is a middle-aged, overweight, self-
indulgent grocer trying to act like a twenty-two-year-old roué. The
result is not identification but rather alienation. Unfortunately this
Jorrocks is exactly the kind of person whom most readers, were they
to meet him in real life, would be tempted to avoid.

For example, when he woos his neighbor, Mrs. Flather, he looks
ridiculous not only to the reader but to Mrs. Flather herself, who
puts up with his advances merely out of boredom or because
tolerating him is sometimes easier or more diplomatic than rejecting
him. Surtees's excuses for Jorrocks's behavior do more to exaggerate
it than to justify it. "Our young readers," he insists, "will turn up
their noses at this . . . but as we get older we get wonderfully
lenient in the matter of age, and see no reason why two old fools
should not amuse themselves as well as two young ones. Besides,"
he continues, "Mrs. Flather was an undespairing widow . . . so
there is nothing improbable, though it may be a little improper, in a
steady old gentleman, like Mr. J., doing as we have described. Well,
right or wrong, J. did it, and but for the encumbrance of Benjamin,
we fear he would have been far worse" (64). Surtees rather misses
the point, however, for it is not Jorrocks's age to which the reader
objects, nor is it necessarily the fact that, although Mrs. Flather
might be a widow, Jorrocks is very much married. What the reader
does object to are Jorrocks's words and actions and attitudes that
brand him as obvious, shallow, insensitive, and patronizing. "Some
might think him a trifle too old; but he thought nothin' o' that, age
was nothin' either in 'osses or women" (69 - 70). " 'Dear me!' said
he, lifting her gown a little . . . 'Werry rum. . . . Never troubles to
look at a woman's face if she's clumsy and beefey about the pins.
*Con*found them long pettikits! There's never no sayin' wot's an under them.' " "Then in an undertone he would indulge in a strong
panegyric on fox'unters, ascribing to them every desirable
matrimonial quality under the sun, which, by a dextrous adaptation
of his subject, he contrived to bend into an exemplification of
himself—Mr. J. was tolerably vain" (71 - 72).

The problem is that this Jorrocks is *in*tolerably vain, and, as a result, when Surtees tries to create situations in this novel similar to those which provide humor in *Handley Cross* , he fails miserably by comparison. Jorrocks of *Handley Cross* climbing out of his bath, cowering wet and shivering behind the door while trying to bluff his way out of a terribly embarrassing situation for which he is not responsible and which catches him completely by surprise, is funny—Jorrocks of *Hillingdon Hall* attacking a gamekeeper at Donkeyton Castle because the man quite naturally assumes that the stranger wandering through the park and gardens is a trespasser is not funny. " 'B—— your imperence!' screamed Mr. Jorrocks, doubling his fists. . . . 'B—— your imperence, I say! you confounded rebellious-looking ruffian, I'll knock you neck and croup in the middle o' the week after next, and spit you like a sparrow afore the fire. Vot do you take me for?' " (80). The difference between the two scenes is that in the latter one Jorrocks has no reason to be abusive: first, he is clearly responsible for his position here whereas in the earlier situation he is a victim of someone else's mistake; and second, a simple revelation of who he is and what he is doing in the park would clear up this misunderstanding, while the difficulty of making plausible excuses for one's taking another man's bath, drinking his liquor, and wearing his clothes might well tempt one to try any expedient short of confession. In the first case Jorrocks reacts more from desperation than from a desire to abuse people; no such excuse can be made for his unwarranted attack in *Hillingdon Hall.* With such incidents as these occurring early in the novel it is not surprising that Jorrocks never does manage to win the reader's confidence or respect. His election to Parliament is much more likely to dismay the reader than to elate him.

One reason why Surtees's failure with his main character in *Hillingdon Hall* is particularly sad is because in many ways this novel is more ambitious than either of the earlier two. In the first place, it moves completely away from the hunting field, for Jorrocks is by now too old to hunt—he goes out once with a pack of harriers and can not keep up the pace. As a result, for the first time Surtees focuses directly on social concerns, the problems of dinner parties and county fairs, of marrying off daughters and winning votes. His area of satire is expanding, and in his next novel he invents a formula even better than that applied in *Handley Cross* to demonstrate both of his favorite parts of society, the hunting field and the country estate. But in Hillingdon Hall he sacrifices the first for the second, and the novel loses vitality as a result.

In the second place, Surtees tries here a more complex plot structure than he had so far attempted. *Jorrocks* is a collection of short
stories; *Handley Cross* is similar in that it remains essentially a
string of loosely connected episodes centering around one locality
and one character. In this third novel, however, Surtees actually introduces two stories instead of just one, and he develops them side
by side throughout the novel. While the adventures of Jorrocks continue to be primarily episodic (his social and political advancements
providing a bit more structure than appeared in *Handley Cross*),
the second story exhibits a full-blown plot. Two rival mothers, Mrs.
Flather and Mrs. Trotter, both try to get their attractive daughters
married to the Marquis of Bray, "and here we may observe that we
believe it to be a well-established fact that every young lady, and
many young ladies' mammas, consider at the outset of life that they
are destined for duchesses" (60 - 61). The Marquis has quite
different ideas, however. "Unfortunately for rival belles, London
beaux . . . consider them a sort of strop to keep the razor of their
palaverment fresh against the return of another London season, and
think they may go to any lengths short of absolutely offering. . . .
The Marquis of Bray was just one of this sort. He knew perfectly
well the Duke would no more think of letting him marry anything
below a Duke's daughter than he would think of sending him off for
a trip in one of Mr. Henson's air carriages; and being well assured
of that fact, he thought the girls must know it also" (94 - 95).

The marquis flirts openly with both girls but goes no further. The
mothers become increasingly desperate. Finally Mrs. Flather, who
feels that she has the most hope because the marquis actually kissed
her Emma, travels to Donkeyton Castle for a showdown. The
duchess assures her "that you are labouring under a strong
delusion. . . . In the first place, in supposing that our son would
ever think of marrying your daughter; and in the second place, in
supposing that the Duke and myself would ever sanction such a
thing" (384). Mrs. Flather is taken aback, but decides, since she has
already compromised her pride by going there, to confront the duke
himself. At first he assumes his son has impregnated the girl, and in
his reaction one can see Surtees's satire at its best. "*It's no use making a row about it—the less said the better* . . . take her abroad—go
on a little tour. . . . I'll pay the expenses. . . . May marry her perhaps—Swiss colonel—Italian count—French general . . . but if you
don't, why, you'll come back at the end of a certain time, and no
one will know anything about it—be any wiser. These sort of things

are unpleasant, no doubt—monstrous unpleasant; but accidents will happen—youthful indiscretion—more cautious in future; sorry for it, I assure you—monstrous sorry for it, but rely upon it, it's no use making a row about it—*hush it up—hush it up*" (392). When he understands that something as serious as marriage is involved, he becomes irate. " 'What? Jeems marry a commoner!—a—a—a—IMPOSSIBLE!' and the Duke stamped as though he would rouse his dormant ancestry to avenge the insult. 'Susan, my dear!' exclaimed he, in a towering passion, 'Mrs. Flather has done us the honour of coming here to claim our son in marriage for her daughter. Compliment! great compliment! monstrous compliment! isn't it?' asked the Duke, white as his whiskers"(393 - 394). Mrs. Flather is mortified, and the story ends with Eliza Trotter marrying Emma's former beau, thus leaving the daughter of the more pushy, ambitious, and conniving mother with nothing. Surtees the social satirist is always obviously Surtees the instructor. There is an interesting footnote to the character of the Duke of Donkeyton; "family tradition has it that Surtees' model for the Duke of Donkeyton was a certain noble neighbour, that the noble neighbour recognised his own portrait, and coolness ensued between the original of Donkeyton Castle and Hamsterley Hall."[33] That "noble neighbour" was none other than the Duke of Northumberland! "The Duke is described in *The Greville Diaries* as 'a very good sort of man, an eternal talker and a prodigious bore,' " Mr. Noakes exclaims, "which certainly sounds like Donkeyton to me."[34]

Unfortunately, Surtees does not always handle these two plots smoothly. Because the characters from the stories interact, they must be synchronized according to time. So when Jorrocks travels off by himself to the county fair, for example, and several chapters and several days are devoted to him, the author finds himself in the awkward situation of having to fill in those days when he switches to the other story. The result is considerable overlapping, for each time Surtees drops one story and picks up the other he feels it necessary to remind the reader of what he has already read. So much of a habit does this become that two-thirds of the way through the novel Surtees pauses to apologize. "We have to apologise to our or Mr. Jorrocks's noble friend, the Marquis of Bray, for the very uncerimonious way we have left him during the last three chapters, dripping in his woman's attire over Mrs. Flather's fire, after the fair Emma disappeared on the announcement of who

he was. It is difficult, in novel-writing," he explains, "to drive the
two parts of the story (into which all orthodox three-volume ones
should be divided) like phaeton horses, and prevent one part out-
stepping the other, and at this point our farmer friend has shot considerably ahead of the ladies" (323). Awkward and sometimes distracting as this device may seem, nevertheless Surtees was trying
something new, something considerably more difficult in terms of
plot and structure than anything he had done before.

The author's intrusion in the above quotation is not inconsistent
with the narrative method of the rest of the novel, for another experiment Surtees tried here was the adoption of an informal tone in
which the author frequently steps outside the story to interpret the
scene, to criticize the characters, to add details or digressions only
loosely related to the story, or simply to move the novel along. For
instance, chapter four actually starts three times. " 'So the new
Squire's come at last!' exclaimed Mrs. Flather, bursting into the
room . . . where Emma sat patching and torturing a piece of
muslin under the pretence of embroidering a collar. Confound
those collars! If women only knew how little men appreciate those
flimsy, fluttering, butterfly articles of dress. . . ." And Surtees is
off on a criticism of collars. Eventually he catches himself; "But to
Mrs. Flather and the Squire. 'So the new Squire's come at last,' was
the exclamation of Mrs. Flather, bursting into the room to her
daughter; and as this is to be a regular orderly three-volume work,
we may as well describe the locality before we proceed." Next, of
course, comes a description of the Flathers' manse, followed by
another attempt to continue the story. "Now, a third time, we will
surely get under weigh. 'So the new Squire's come at last!' exclaimed Mrs. Flather to her daughter' " (12 - 13).

When describing the character of Bill Dowker, social gadfly,
Surtees suggests that his position of theater critic "brought him, of
course, a good deal among actresses, and we have heard that several
of his 'How d'ye do!' great acquaintance arose out of little delicate
arrangements that he had the felicity of bringing about." Then, in
the manner of a true gossip, he cautions, "This, however, we don't
vouch for; we will therefore thank our readers not to 'quote us' on
this point" (22 - 23). In another place he reports that Emma actually had her head on the Marquis's shoulder, but hastens to add, "As
a justice would say—that may, or may not be—it may be true, or it
may be a lie—it may be Betsey's lie—it may be Benjamin's lie—or
it may be the boy in button's lie—it may be true and yet have
nothing in it" (205).

Some of his advice, on the other hand, is very practical indeed. After describing how a country gentleman may be forced to sell a horse to provide his daughter a season in London for the purpose of attracting a wealthy husband, Surtees asks, "What does he see when he gets to London? Why, that every other girl he meets with is quite as good, and many a deuced deal better-looking than Jemima. Take an author's advice, Brown, and stay at home" (93). Another time he warns, "Fair ladies; beware of the small talk of young gentlemen in cerulean blue satin waistcoats worked with heart's-ease, and pink pantaloons"(117).

Halfway through the book the author stops to reveal his own in-adequacy.

A rather difficult passage in our history now draws near—namely, what the ladies did when they got back to the drawing-room at Donkeyton Castle. In these points authors disclose their sex. A lady would be *great* here, whereas we of the breeches, at least *legitimately* of the breeches, are "quite out." In this dilemma we inquired of a female friend . . . what ladies did when they retired from the dining-room. "Oh," said she, "they generally go to the fire, dawdle and stand about a little, and then sit down and talk scandal." We will then, gentle reader, with your permission, suppose the fire, and standing about part done, and that the ladies are pairing off, or gouping for the scandal stakes (104).

Another time he takes the liberty to "think our indulgent readers will acquit us of taxing their credulity beyond the stretch of literary latitudinarianship" (117).

Usually these asides and digressions, unless they are merely functional in directing the story, tie in well with Surtees's satire, for they give him a chance to emphasize or clarify a point that is more subtly expressed in the story itself. For example, after describing throughout the book the endless toasts at dinner parties, he pauses in the middle of the toasts at the county fair dinner to exclaim, "Thank God! farmers are no orators. They are almost the only class exempt from the curse of eloquence. They say what they've got to say, and are done with it, instead of yammering and 'honourable-friend-ing' 'honourable-gentlemaning,' and moving, seconding, amending, using all the jargon of Parliament, in fact" (309).

Considering that this is the first time Surtees has tried this technique, he handles it well. Rather than detracting from the story, his comments add another, personal dimension. He must have been pleased himself with the result, for he continues the experiment in his next novel, *Hawbuck Grange*, only in that novel the intrusions become more frequent, longer, and less relevant, and the story is

neither strong nor interesting enough to withstand such tampering.
Later still, in *Ask Mamma*, he makes the same mistake. But in
Hillingdon Hall the balance between the narrative intrusions and
the stories themselves is carefully controlled, and the result is often
delightful.

There is one more point, of biographical interest, to be made
about *Hillingdon Hall*, and that is the extent to which it reveals
Surtees's agrarian and political interests. It is because of its
enlightened presentation of farming techniques that Watson
describes it as "knowledgeable," calling it, in fact, "a handbook to
the farmer's progress."[35] Surtees farmed The Hagg, 250 acres,
himself, managed seven hundred acres of woodland, and kept a
herd of thirty cattle. His personal interest in the farming aspect of
his estate is clearly indicated by the number of notebook entries he
made to remind him of "a gate to be repaired, turnips to be rolled,
so many loads of manure to be led to this field or that, drains to be
cleared, rat-traps to be ordered, tar to be bought."[36] Sixteen years
after this novel, in 1861, he was to write an account of Durham
farming which, according to Cooper, "shows that during those
twenty three years Surtees had studied deeply and with sympathy
the problems of the Durham agriculturist, especially of the small
farmer. . . . The 'Description of Durham' contains a careful
analysis of the difficulties that faced the small farmer in the district,
shortage of capital, uncertainty of leases and the Repeal of the Corn
Laws being the principal. It deals too with the question of land
drainage and land fertilization, which were pet hobbies of Surtees
and by descent from him of Mr. Jorrocks."[37]

While he favored experimentation and scientific progress,
however, Surtees had contempt for what Watson calls "the get-rich-
quick schemes of reckless innovations."[38] Surtees himself makes the
distinction clear in his preface to *Hillingdon Hall*. "The author of
the work will not trespass on the indulgence of the reader, in the
way of preface, further than to say that the agricultural portion of it
is not meant to discourage improvement, but to repress the wild
schemes of theoretical men, who attend farmers' meetings for the
pleasure of hearing themselves talk, and do more harm than good
by the promulgation of their visionary views" (preface). Hence
Jorrocks brags at a farmers' meeting about his "monster reaper"
which he has no real intention of ever trying to create and his new
draining tile which he has never tried to produce. He is actually
dumbfounded when Pigg, who acts in this novel as Jorrocks's

overseer, tells him that one of his tenants "won't clean his land; and he'll say, thou tell'd him not, and that he kept it to try thy engine on"(357), and that another tenant is buying huge quantities of sugar to make the new tiles. " 'Oh dear! Mr. 'Eavytail must be a werry stupid man,' observed Mr. Jorrocks, wondering how a tenant of his could have fallen into a trap he had only set for other people"(355). Surtees "had no time for gentlemen playing at being farmers who tried to use 'science' as a short cut instead of getting down to it and learning their job thoroughly," insists Mr. Noakes. "His instinctive preference for the professional over the amateur . . . would not allow him to let even his fond creation Jorrocks make the transition from grocer to farmer a tale of unqualified success."[39] "It is a mistake to suppose that any fool will make a farmer," warns Jorrocks. "A farmer should be a philosopher, an astrologer, a chemist, an engineer, a harchitect, a doctor, I don't know what else"(155). He has learned the lesson the hard way, for in a moment of sober honesty he is heard to exclaim, "Vish I was a *real* farmer instead of one of those harm-chair 'umbugs—*pheelo*siphers what they call"(263).

His dedication to farming made Surtees naturally a supporter of the Corn Laws, and his fear that England's lifting the heavy taxes on imported wheat would destroy the farmer and endanger the nation is clearly evident in Jorrocks's election speeches. "I've been brought here," he explains on nomination day, "by a great lot o' farmers; they came and 'unted me out at my 'ouse at 'ome, and would have me. . . . I never axed to be made Parliament man of. The farmers came and said that they were like to be beggared, and axed if I would stand quietly by and see 'em?" To the argument that lowering the price on imported wheat would lower the cost of bread and thereby help the poor, Jorrocks points out that farmers facing markets flooded with foreign wheat would not be able to sell their produce, and the inevitable result would be greater unemployment and more poverty. "It sounds werry well talking about bein' the poor man's friend, but I say he is the best poor man's friend wot gives him a good day's pay for a good day's work. Vot signifies it to the poor man gettin' a heightpenny loaf for fourpence if he has not fourpence to buy it with?" He brings the argument closer to home by using one of his own tenants as an example."Then I would like to ax my noble friend 'ow he thinks to improve the breed o' the 'uman race, if he makes us poor farmers lay our land down to grass or pine-apples, throwin' the corn-trade into the hands of

mouncheer, and drivin' the chaws into mills and print-works. . . .
Wot 'un a man would Mr. 'Eavytail ha' been if he'd been brought
up a shuttle-weaver?" From the local scene he switches to the
future national implication of repeal. "Who knows but the Prince
de Johnville or Prince de Tomville, or whatever they call the chap,
may brew up another storm, and in the row and racket that ensues,
who knows but another Napoleon le grand may turn to the top,
who'll swear that we shalln't 'ave another grain o' corn from the
Continent? Then, gen'lmen, if you've laid your land down to grass,
and turned your stout yeomanry into stockin' makers, who's to
supply us with bread?" (504 - 506). These speeches may come from
the lips of Jorrocks, but they originated in the heart of Surtees.

Reviewed in its entirety, *Hillingdon Hall* is not a bad book, certainly not a "slough of dullness." In fact, those readers who receive
their introduction to Surtees and Jorrocks through this novel will
probably consider it a good book. The fact that it is in some respects
inferior to the other novels of the trilogy is offset by the realization
that it is also the most ambitious. Surtees's experimentation with
this novel, his fumbling and uncertain striving to find and develop
his own mature voice and style, together with the biographical in-
sights it affords and the good humor provided by many of the
characters and situations, make *Hillingdon Hall* a novel worth the
attention of those who love Jorrocks and admire Surtees.

CHAPTER 3

Tom Scott and Soapey Sponge

I Hawbuck Grange

"What queer books you write!" observed our excellent but rather matter-of-fact friend, Sylvanus Bluff, the other day, who seeing us doubling up a sheet of paper in a rather unceremonious way, concluded we were at what he calls our "old tricks." "I buy all your books," added he . . . "I bought your 'Jorrocks' Jaunts and Jollities,' I bought 'Handley Cross, or the Spa Hunt,' I bought 'Hillingdon Hall, or the Cockney Squire'; but I don't *understand* them. I don't see the *wit* of them. *I* don't see the *use* of them. *I* wonder you don't write something useful. I should think now," added he seriously, "you could do something better. I should say now you would be quite equal to writing a dictionary, or a book upon draining, and those would be really useful works, and your friends would get something for their money."[1]

IT is ironic that Surtees should choose *Hawbuck Grange,* one of his least successful novels, to have this bit of fun with himself, and that he should do so toward the *end* of that novel, when one would expect him to be most blind to its defects, says something in favor of his literary judgment. "Gentle reader! we plead guilty to the charge of writing most egregious nonsense. Nay, we are sometimes surprised how such stuff can ever enter our head, astonished that we should be weak enough tò commit it to paper, amazed that there should be publishers rash enough to print it, and lost in utter bewilderment that there should be good, honest, sane, nay sensible folks not only idle enough to read it, but, oh wonder! of all wonders! extravagant enough to part with their good current coin to buy it!"(237). Certainly his earlier novels do not deserve such harsh treatment except in fun; unfortunately, one cannot say the same for *Hawbuck Grange.* Surtees might well have sensed this, for he carries his apology further. "Writing, we imagine, is something like snuffing or smoking—men get in the way of it, and can't well leave it off. Like smoking, it serves to beguile an idle hour"(238).

"To beguile an idle hour" must have been Surtees's primary reason for writing this book; his secondary reason was to provide a kind of memorial to November 1846, "the worst hunting November that perhaps ever was known"(48). "Our friend Bluff's reproof has made us anxious to give this volume a flavour of usefulness, were it only to save us from the labour of writing a dictionary" he explains. "In the course of our cogitations, it has occurred to us that the only possible way of doing it is to give a sort of meteorological register of the season in which our friend Tom Scott's adventures are laid"(239 - 240). Indeed, one could almost consider the weather to be the book's protagonist—as for its being the antagonist, there can be no question. "What an apology of a season it was! What a hope-raising, spirit-crushing affair all through!"(240). After reading the many striking descriptions of sleet, fog, bitter cold, mud, frost, run-ny noses, red hands, and frozen feet, the reader is inclined to agree. "There's more English weather in Surtees than any where I know, except England,"[2] jokes Mr. Renwick.

Certainly to write a successful novel covering only one month's time would require a great deal of skill and planning. One would expect to find a strong central character in whom the reader is truly interested, a plot of some complexity that can be developed quickly and concisely and brought soon to a climax, a cast of supporting characters who are easily identifiable and essential to the story, a careful control of time, including a discriminating use of flashbacks. *Hawbuck Grange* has none of these. Mr. Cooper summarizes and critiques the novel in one sentence: "It is the most loosely con-structed of all Surtees's works, and is really little more than a number of isolated incidents, more or less bound together by the presence at all of them of the pleasant but uninteresting Tom Scott."[3] He goes on to say that "it is a sad piece of amateur carpen-try, and the joints creak and gape in an alarming fashion. There is no plot at all. . . . It is like a cake composed of the finest and richest ingredients which the cook has forgotten to mix. There are plums in it in plenty and sugar with a spice of vinegar. But the dough is indigestible."[4] Aubrey Noakes, in his entire book on Surtees, awards this novel just two sentences. "It was not successful," he writes, "and perhaps did not deserve to be. Its hero, Mr. Thomas Scott, is not a very interesting character."[5]

It is intriguing to speculate why, after three novels bursting with Jorrocks, Surtees created Tom Scott as the hero of his fourth book. Perhaps he merely desired a change; perhaps he wanted to find out if he could write successfully about another kind of person, far different not only from Jorrocks but also from all the minor characters in his earlier novels. Or perhaps he was reacting to outside influences—none of the earlier novels had been particularly successful, and with Sholbert's command to "prune down a little of the coarseness of the fox-hunting grocer" still in his memory, he might have hoped a Tom Scott would prove more to the public's liking. Mr. Cuming quotes a revealing letter to Surtees from his friend Robert Ingham which demonstrates the kind of criticism the author was receiving: "There is only one defect which I should like to hint at. Why not make your satire effective by restraint? Do give us a *good* character, man or woman; honest, truthful, domestic, trying to do what duty requires to God and man, and happy accordingly. You are only in your first number and you could easily weave one golden thread in your fabric."[6] This comment, it is true, was written in respect to *Ask Mamma*, a much later novel, but it is indicative of the kind of pressure Surtees was under. If Tom Scott were "one golden thread" in *Hawbuck Grange* he might, indeed, have been a welcome addition; unfortunately, he is the whole cloth!

"Surtees apparently decided to have a normal human being for a hero for once,"[7] writes Cooper, but if Tom Scott is "normal," then the majority of the human race must be very dull. Siegfried Sassoon goes even further. "I have a special affection for Thomas Scott," he writes, "since he is one of the few unquestionably likeable characters in Surtees, charming, sensible and modest, and—in my opinion—the nearest to a self-portrait in his works."[8] The very fact that *Hawbuck Grange* exists at all is sufficient refutation of Sassoon's identification of a self-portrait—Tom Scott lacks both imagination and ambition to undertake a novel, except perhaps in fireside musings, and to complete not one but eight novels and several other works besides is entirely beyond his capacity. Besides, Surtees—with his wife and three children, his financially successful country estate, his numerous positions of responsibility in his community, his political involvement and local lectures, his fighting on behalf of his poorer neighbors and inmates of workhouses, his connections with the literary world—was actively and intimately involved with life. Poor Tom Scott could not even manage to get himself married! Fortunately Surtees was *not* a Tom Scott, and the world is a much happier place for it.

Tom Scott has no spirit. He is polite almost to the point of hypocrisy, suffering silently under the absurdities and insults of

Tarquinius Muff, "Scott's abomination"(5). The one time he does
talk back to Muff he is not very effective. "*You* know I know
something about hunting, Tom Scott," Muff challenges him.
" '*Indeed I don't*,' replied Tom, nettled at his meanness, and unable to resist the temptation of having a shy at him. 'Not about fox-
hunting, at all events,' continued Scott, thinking to qualify his
answer"(35). On another occasion, at the end of an excellent run
with the harriers of the Goose and Dumpling hunt, Scott pleads for
the hare's life. " 'To be, or not to be,' was the question,—a live hare
or a dead one. '*Save her!*' whispered Scott, 'save her! she's a good-
un, and will give us a gallop another day. Mercy's all that's wanting
to make the day's sport perfect' "(39). There is nothing wrong, of
course, in showing mercy to the hunted hare, but the sentiment is so
far from what Jorrocks would feel and so foreign to Surtees's
previous writing experience that, taken with the rest of Scott's
character, it sounds more insipid than compassionate. Tom Scott is
seldom capable of a strong emotion of any kind. When he visits
Lord Lazytongs, son of the Marquis of Fender and Fireirons, and
misses the hunt because his host oversleeps, overbreakfasts, and
changes his neckcloth at the last minute because his wife disap-
proves of it, Tom is seriously provoked but careful not to show it.
"Poor Tom was never so vexed in his life! He could have cried, if no
one had been there." Significantly, though, he neither cries nor
makes any complaint except for muttering, "All that hanged
neckcloth!"(94) under his breath.

The only time Tom could be accused of doing anything the least
bit questionable is when he is virtually forced by some friends to
take advantage of the gullibility of the "cretur," Toe Tugtail, who
makes himself obnoxious by fawning over everyone of any importance. "I say, Scott, old Boy," Gurney Sadlad hails him, "they've
been hoaxing the 'cretur' that you are the Duke of Devonshire, and
we want you to carry on the joke." Tom hesitates at first, not on
moral grounds but because "*I* can't personate the Duke of Devonshire, a man I never saw in my life." After the phony introduction is
made Tom tries to break away from Tugtail. "Vain hope! Whenever
Tom turned, the 'cretur' was at his heels; worse still, the crowd
followed to hear the fun. How he did be-duke, and be-grace and be-
lord him!" Scott finally falls in with the fun, telling Tugtail how he
is going to "substitute peacocks, ostriches, cassiowaries, and other
eastern birds, for our common-place pheasants and partridges," and
how he plans either to remodel his estate, "Orientalize the whole

thing, and combine every English comfort with Eastern magnificence," or to "buy the Pavilion at Brighton, and place it on the site of the present house"(224 - 229). While most of Surtees's characters, and, indeed, Surtees himself (the author once introduced Nimrod to a field of fox-hunters as a London merchant who had never been out with the hounds before), would either have initiated this plot against the "cretur" themselves or have gone along with it happily, Scott, of course, is conscience-stricken, and because he is Scott he must suffer for his sin. Four years later he again meets the "cretur," this time in the company of Tarquinius Muff who knows very well who Tom is. Tugtail insists that "when I first saw you, I abso*lutely* took you for my friend the Duke of Devonshire." Tom's self-conscious denials are to no avail, however, for the mere resemblance is enough to encourage the tiresome Tugtail to spend the rest of the day with Tom. "So the 'cretur' persecuted poor Tom from cover to cover, throughout a long blank day," moralizes Surtees, "who declares that if everybody suffers as much for telling a lie as he did, he's sure they won't tell any more"(234 - 236).

Tom's lack of character is best illustrated by his courtship, for he supposedly, for *nine years*, has been contemplating marriage to a Miss Lydia Clifton; the fact that the young woman never appears in the novel symbolizes well the lack of substance in Tom's feeling for her. His priorities are clearly demonstrated after an unsuccessful day of hunting when he returns "cold, dejected, cheerless, dispirited, and chilled" to "his solitary home." Lounging in his easy chair before the fire he muses, "Hunting has been the balm and charm of my youth . . . but hang it, if this November is to be taken as a sample of what's to come, it's precious little use persevering in the line. . . . Poor Lydia Clifton! If it hadn't been for this hunting I'd have married you long since." Sneezing under the influence of an impending cold, he calls for a foot bath and decides, "I really think I'll give up hunting and marry her still, for it's no use keeping horses for such work as this"(55 - 56). He calls on her occasionally when he's in the neighborhood, but "he carried on the courtship more by 'innuendo' than by the old point blank, 'If you love me as I love you,' &c. Indeed, to tell the truth, Tom is rather a cautious cock, and thought if he could but get his own consent, that of the lady would follow as a matter of course"(162). Twice he is close to proposing, but on the first occasion the weather is so bad he decides not to go out (57), and the second time, when he is bored and lonely

at a terrible country inn, he is distracted from his task of writing a
proposal when he comes across a letter that reminds him of a certain
hunt which he must immediately run over in detail in his mind.
"Oh, this hunting! this hunting! what a deal it has to answer for"
(109), mourns Surtees. No one but Tom is surprised by the letter he
receives from Lydia at the end of the novel thanking him for his
"fatherly interest" and informing him that she is about to marry her
cousin. No reader can feel very sorry for Tom Scott!

Fortunately *Hawbuck Grange* has more to offer than one main
character; it is essentially a collection of hunting episodes made up
of revisions of various sporting articles which appeared irregularly
in *Bell's Life* between October 1846 and June 1847. It is primarily
the framework for these sketches that is weak, for once Surtees is in
the middle of a chase his writing is every bit as good as it was in
Handley Cross. Here Surtees displays the respect he feels for all
kinds and methods of hunting so long as they are done well. Squire
Neville is his ideal sportsman, drawn as he was from the character of
Ralph Lambton, a man of twenty-three years' experience, "one of
the last of the old school of sportsmen; of men who made fox-
hunting their study, instead of mixing it up with half-a-dozen other
pursuits. Everything connected with his establishment is ordered
with the regularity of the army, and conducted with the precision of
a regiment. . . . Year after year has seen him the same. . . . His
hair may be a shade greyer, whiter rather; but his figure retains its
pristine lightness and neatness, he sits well into his saddle, and looks
like what he is—a gentleman and a sportsman" (6 - 7). For contrast
Surtees also describes a field of inferior men.

Fox-hunting should be done handsomely! There is something about the noble animal that forbids our treating him slightingly. He should be hunted
like a gentleman. What chance have a lot of trencher-fed, milk-fattened,
street-scouring beggars with a good high-couraged, clean-feeding, well-
conditioned flyer? None whatever! . . . Nothing can be more pitiable
than the half-rigged turn out of an ill-supported pretension to a fox-hunt.
The boosey-looking huntsman (generally the saddler or publican)—the
wretched broken-kneed, over-worked leg-weary job horse—the jaded half
jockey, half huntsman-looking caps—the seedy, misfitting, Holywell-street-
looking coats—the unclean boots and filthy breeches—with the lamentable
apologies for saddles and bridles. We never see a Tom-and Jerry-looking
"scarlet" without thinking how much more respectable the wearer would
look in black. We never see a country-scouring, fence-flattening field
without thinking how much better they would be with a pack of harriers
(14, 17).

Despite that innuendo against harriers, however, they come in for their share of praise in this novel, especially in the Goose and Dumpling Hunt, "in which the whole art and craft of hare-hunting," writes Watson, "is taken at leisure, and with that pleasant air of smiling but knowledgeable approbation with which Surtees always wrote about harriers."[9] One is reminded that Surtees grew up hunting hare as well as fox at Hamsterley, and although most of his fox-hunting readers thought of hare-hunting as a second-rate sport, he refused to share their snobbery. Speaking of the Goose and Dumpling Hunt Surtees writes, "Indeed, the hounds are as good as can be, and have been in existence nearly forty years, during the whole of which time the greatest care and attention have been paid to their breeding. . . . The members of the hunt are all real sportsmen, men who love hunting innately, but who take no pleasure in leaping. . . . Some people fancy hard riding an indispensable quality for a sportsman; but we believe, if we were to canvass the sporting world, we should find that the real lovers of hunting are anything but a hard-riding set. Fond of seeing hounds work, they use their horses as a sort of auxiliary to their legs"(19 - 20). As Cooper points out, "It is Surtees's old creed; the hound rather than the horse, the hunt than the gallop, the gap or gate than the fence. It is the hunting of Anthony Surtees at Hamsterley."[10]

Another tribute to Hamsterley can be seen in the Stout-as-Steel pack which hunts country so hilly and difficult that the master and hunt servants are mounted on mules and follow the course of the hounds with telescopes; hunting with these hounds makes Scott, who has an inclination to laugh when he first sees the strange procession, wish he had a mule himself. The country around Hamsterley might not have been quite that severe, but as Watson says, with the "description of this most business-like hill pack Surtees was obviously not simply at home, but imbued with all the pride of his own country."[11]

Good and numerous as the hunting scenes are, however, they cannot, unsupported, carry the novel, and *Hawbuck Grange* has little more to offer. In fact its defects quite overshadow its good points. For one thing, Surtees carried further in this novel his experiment in author-intrusion which he started in *Hillingdon Hall.* Perhaps he had Sterne's *Tristram Shandy* in mind as a model; unfortunately, he lacked Sterne's genius, and the result is complete confusion between Tom Scott's story and the author's digressions, between the third person and the first, between the present and the past. Sometimes these digressions are meant to be educational, as when he points out that "good farming is certainly a great promoter of hunting" (198), or "wet is not indispensable to scent" (258), or "a horse's coat furnishes a pretty good criterion of the state of the atmosphere" (185), or even when he insists that "there is nothing makes a person look so queer as an extremely long frock or great-coat" (18). Other times he pauses to carry on a conversation with the reader, much in imitation of Sterne. Chapter nine, for example, begins in this distracting way: " 'WHO-OOP!' 'Who-oop! That's a queer way of beginning a chapter, Mr. Author!' 'So it is, Mr. Reader, but you'll have a good many more of them before you are done' "(134). Sterne's great antinovel is composed entirely of such literary devices; unfortunately Surtees's few sorry attempts irritate the reader rather than amuse him.

Undoubtedly the weakest parts of the novel are chapters thirteen and fourteen. Cooper says of them, "It would be a great improvement to the book if Chapters XIII to XV were cut out altogether as they have no bearing on the story and are unworthy of their author."[12] Chapter thirteen, entitled "A Blank Day," is a clumsy flashback to Tom's experiences four years earlier when he traveled to Fast-and-Loose Castle to hunt with the Duke of Tergiversation's hounds. Surtees satirizes the pomposity of the Prince of Spankenhausen, Mynhher Von Cled, and "several other great Dutch swells" (204), and describes the confusion created by hundreds of people crowding around to see the celebrities, as well as the absurdity of the little hatter Billy Bobbinson and his inept guard of honor made up of local yeomanry. The chapter is significant only in its biographical interest, for the Prince of Spankenhausen is based on Baron Gablenz, that strange Saxon whom Surtees had met in Brighton eighteen years before, and the charge of the "bold dragoons" after the fox was undoubtedly inspired by Surtees's experiences with the gendarmes in Boulogne. The foxes are, of course, bagged ("They are going to turn down a brace of things on the other side of the hill that have been in a sack these three days, poor things," confides huntsman to Lord—216), and the first one is caught in a rabbit trap and the second quickly killed by the hounds before he can break away. A drag is made of the body of one of the dead animals, however, and, pulled behind a horse out of sight of the field, serves just as well to please the uninitiated. This farce over, Surtees makes matters worse by pretending to have played a trick on the reader with the chapter title and explaining the joke to him in a most condescending manner. " 'Well, but where's your

blank?' we fancy we hear the reader say. 'You've killed a brace of
foxes! how's that? that's no blank!' Gentle reader, we admit it; it
wouldn't be a blank to some, but it was to Lord Harkaway and
many of the gentlemen who 'harkaway' with him. Will you,
however, take it seriously amiss if we tell you that all this is merely
preliminary to the 'blank day'? We hope not, for unless you close
the book, you have all your medicine yet to take"(219 - 220).

Chapter fourteen, "The Blank Day—(*continued*)," picks up the
story where the previous chapter had left off four years before the
present time of the novel, describes Tom's first encounter with the
"cretur" Toe Tugtail, jumps suddenly ahead in time three years
(not four) and tells about Tom's second meeting with Tugtail and
the *real* "blank day." At the end Surtees gloats, "Now, if that isn't a
blank day, we don't know what a blank day is"(236). The chapters
are confusing, the transition of time is handled badly, the first-
person comments are snide rather than clever, and the experience of
reading these two chapters is irritating and, for fans of Surtees, extremely disappointing. Susan Hallgarth examines Surtees's applica-
tion of theatrical techniques in his novels, and suggests that what he
is doing in this novel is assuming the role of "scene-shifter." While
the technique was innovative at the time and was employed
(although usually to a much lesser degree) throughout all Surtees's
novels, when carried to this extreme "such intrusions tend to distance author and reader from the characters and scenes, and
whether he invites his audience to participate in a scene or merely
to watch it, neither he nor his audience becomes totally involved."[13]

So if *Hawbuck Grange* is to be considered, as it might well be,
another experiment by Surtees in creating new types of characters
and trying new methods of storytelling, it has to be judged an experiment that fails. With what relief the reader picks up *Mr.
Sponge's Sporting Tour* and finds himself back in that Surteesian
style of *Handley Cross!*

II   Mr. Sponge's Sporting Tour

Soapey Sponge is as different from Tom Scott as any two people
can be from one another. To the extent that Scott is a very moral
man, Sponge is a complete rogue. Surtees himself evidently felt a
little uncomfortable with Sponge, and well he might have. "Victorian novelists found it so extremely precarious to write about unpleasant, dishonest, or otherwise regrettable persons, unless to point

an improving moral, that even Surtees shrank perceptibly from Sponge. . . . The most approved novelists, whether they were Dickens or Mrs. Gaskell or Charles Reade, were full of social uplift."[14] Watson asks about Surtees, "As a middle-aged, married man, a Justice of the Peace, a staunch Churchman, and so forth, how could he discover any artistic, respectable, or ethical message in Soapey Sponge?"[15] The answer is that he could not, for Sponge is completely incorrigible, and any "uplift" the reader gets from the book is in the area of delightful entertainment, not enlightening morality. The fact that Surtees made any effort, however halfhearted, to attach a "moral" to such a novel and such a character proves that he was indeed a product of his age. His preface, obviously written after he had completed the book and could find no Victorian justification for its existence, is half explanation, half apology. "The author gladly avails himself," he writes, "of the convenience of a Preface for stating, that it will be seen at the close of the work why he makes such a characterless character as Mr. Sponge the hero of his tale. He will be glad if it serves to put the rising generation on their guard against specious, promiscuous acquaintance, and trains them on to the noble sport of hunting, to the exclusion of its mercenary, illegitimate off-shoots."[16] The lack of seriousness is obvious here, for the "close of the work" illustrates, if anything, the advantages of a life of vice—Sponge marries the beautiful heroine and settles down in London with a successful tobacco shop and betting room, seemingly happier and more affluent than he has ever been in his life. As Watson jokes, "Surtees as a moralist has never been handed round to Sunday-school scholars."[17] That problem aside, then, the reader is free to look at *Mr. Sponge* as good humor rather than as good morality.

By far the outstanding feature of this novel is its superb characterization, and Soapey Sponge himself leads a pack of creatures so peculiar, so intriguingly original, sometimes so repulsive and sometimes so endearing, that they must rank in effectiveness with those of Dickens.

The hero of the book, Mr. Sponge, has two strong prejudices: he hates work and he despises poverty. And while he is never seen to indulge in the first, he also manages to avoid the second, for he is a con-artist superb, a very "soapey sponge" indeed!

Mr. Sponge was a good-looking, rather vulgar-looking man. At a distance—say ten yards—his height, figure, and carriage gave him somewhat of a commanding appearance, but this was rather marred by a jerky, twitchy, uneasy sort of air, that too plainly showed he was not the natural, or what the lower orders call the *real* gentleman. Not that Sponge was shy. Far from it. He never hesitated about offering to a lady, after three days' acquaintance, or in asking a gentleman to take him a horse in over-night, with whom he might chance to come in contact in the hunting-field. And he did it all in such a cool, off-hand, matter-of-course sort of way, that people who would have stared with astonishment if anybody else had hinted at such a proposal, really seemed to come into the humour and spirit of the thing, and to look upon it rather as a matter of course than otherwise (2 - 3).

Surtees further explains that "Mr. Sponge knew what he was about. . . . He knew there were places where a man can follow up the effect produced by a red coat in the morning to great advantage in the evening; and if he couldn't hunt every day in the week, as he could have wished, he felt he might fill up his time quite as profitably in other ways" (16). The "other ways" with which he fills up his time consist primarily of trading horses to his own advantage and getting himself invited as a nonpaying guest into other people's homes—and staying there. He is eminently successful at both.

His horse-trading activities are masterfully planned to involve no risk to himself. Occasionally these deals become quite complex, as in the case of the sale of Hercules to Mr. Waffles. What is especially important about this particular incident is that Surtees appears to have become so enthusiastic with the intricacies of Sponge's dastardly scheme that he almost lost control of his main character, a rare lapse in his otherwise remarkable critical judgment.

Essential to his error here is the character of Mr. Waffles, an excellent example of one of Surtees's favorite character types, the gullible pseudo-dandy. Waffles "was just in the hey-day of hot, rash, youthful indiscretion and extravagance. He had not the slightest idea of the value of money, and looked at the fortune he was so closely approaching as perfectly inexhaustible" (18 - 19). A "pretty man" (19), he has a high opinion of himself, and when in the hunting field "his tongue was never at fault. It was jabber, jabber, jabber; chatter, chatter, chatter; prattle, prattle; occasionally about something, oftener about nothing, but in cover or out, stiff country or open, trotting or galloping, wet day or dry, good scenting day or bad, Waffles' clapper never was at rest" (20). He is proud and rash and naive; as Mr. Watson says, "Waffles would have tempted a bishop, if only for his organ fund."[18] He is, of course, the perfect victim for the devious and cool Mr. Sponge, and Surtees was so pleased with this perfect match that he has Sponge bilk Waffles not once, but twice, and in this overexuberance lies the problem, for that second swindle shows Sponge in his worst light.

After managing to sell Hercules, a fine-looking but vicious animal, to the prideful and overeager Waffles, Sponge first waits until his victim has discovered the true character of the beast and then sends one of his city friends to buy the horse back, naturally at a substantial loss to poor Waffles, who is every bit as anxious now to unload him as he was previously to buy him. As if all that were not enough, Sponge takes that extra, critical step, and it is at this point that the reader objects. He blackmails Waffles by threatening a lawsuit in the name of Hercules's original owner, from whom Sponge was supposed to have purchased him in the first place, if the horse is not immediately returned so reparation can be made for his viciousness. Faced with this threat, Waffles is only too happy to pay Sponge still more money for what he believes to be an out-of-court settlement.

Throughout all this, Surtees does nothing whatsoever to soften Sponge's character. Upon receiving this second payment from Waffles, Sponge feels nothing but elation. "At first Mr. Sponge was overjoyed. It would set him up for the season. He thought how he'd spend it." His second thought is far different from what the reader of Victorian novels expects. " 'Confound it!' exclaimed Sponge, 'I don't do myself justice! *I'm too much of a gentleman!* I should have had five 'under'd—such an ass as Waffles deserves to be done!' " (64). Whether Sponge thinks Waffles "deserves to be done" or not is rather beside the point; the reader wonders whether Waffles "deserves to be done" to quite this extent. Although he is a proud, loud-mouthed, obnoxious bore, even Surtees insists that "still he was a rattling, good-natured, harum-scarum fellow" (21), and although he can well afford to lose the money, still his youth and ingenuous character argue for a bit of mercy. Surtees and Sponge show none.

It is true that Surtees's primary rogues—Jorrocks, Sponge, Romford—take advantage only of other people's willingness, in fact, anxiousness, to be deceived, thus maintaining a kind of moral integrity. As Mr. Noakes says about Sponge, "His victims are seen to fall a prey to their own cupidity and hopes as much as to the wiles of Soapey."[19] That accounts, certainly, for the initial sale of Hercules; had Waffles not been so anxious to own a horse better than that owned by anyone else, he would not have made the deal. He was deceived by his own foolish pride. But Sponge's taking advantage of the young man the second time, when his pride and impetuosity have already been publicly exposed, seems to be going a bit too far. This is all Sponge's doing—Waffles is no longer the willing victim, and the reader is surely inclined to take Waffles's part, to the detriment of the character of the hero. Fortunately for Surtees this incident takes place toward the beginning of the novel and the author is able to salvage his hero by never again allowing him to sink to this low level of rascality. It is a good thing, for had Sponge been allowed to continue in the character he displays here, Surtees would undoubtedly have alienated his readers. Mr. Johnston-Jones notes this same essential change in the direction of the novel, but he sees it as arising not from the author's almost losing control of his plot but rather from a genuine change in Surtees's attitude toward his character as Sponge developed. "Whereas in Chapter 1 he is at pains to point out that Sponge is no gentleman, by Chapter 9 he is emphasizing his skill and courage on horseback. From now on we hear more and more about Sponge's good qualities and correspondingly less about his bad ones."[20] For whatever reason Surtees made the change, one must respect his critical judgment when he transforms Sponge from a first-class villain into a pertinacious pest.

For the rest of the novel Sponge's most engaging quality is just that—engaging himself to dine, engaging himself to hunt, engaging himself to stay. In fact, "his dexterity in getting into people's houses was only equalled by the difficulty of getting him out again" (3). It is at this activity that he truly earns the name "Sponge." Here Surtees has hit upon the perfect vehicle for his satire, for as Sponge moves from house to house and from hunting field to hunting field Surtees can bring together again, as he had to a lesser degree in *Handley Cross*, his two favorite settings for satirizing the absurdity of human nature, the hunting field and country society. To illustrate these absurdities the author arranges for Sponge to encounter in his varied adventures an absolutely incredible collection of fakes and dandies and humbugs of all kinds, all of whom make Sponge look good by comparison—which is, of course, the point of the novel. Thus the reader has constantly before him the direct contrast of Surtees's natural and his artificial men.

Sponge's first visit, for instance, is to Mr. Jawleyford, a "great humbug. He was a fine, off-hand, open-hearted, cheery sort of fellow, who was always delighted to see you. . . . Though he

never gave dinners, nor anything where he was, he asked
everybody, at least everybody who did give them, to visit him at
Jawleyford Court" (65 - 66). His extending of invitations, which
were, of course, never acted upon, has become so much a habit with
him that he makes the fatal mistake of inviting Sponge, along with
most of the population of Laverick Wells, to Jawleyford Court.
Sponge really believes the sincerity of the invitation and decides to
accept, especially since free lodging, free food, free keep for his
horses, plenty of free hunting, and the presence of two marriageable
Jawleyford daughters are temptations he cannot afford to pass by.
Poor Jawleyford never expected such a thing, and although he
assumes that Sponge is wealthy merely because the man talks and
hunts like a person of wealth, he still makes a single gesture of
defiance in refusing to board Sponge's horses. This bit of independence makes matters worse, for Sponge declares revenge.
"Confounded screw! I'll *work* him for it," he vows. "He sha'n't get
rid of *me* in a hurry," and then adds what will be his continuing
creed, "at least not unless I can get a better billet elsewhere" (72).

Life at Jawleyford Court is, in the beginning, everything Sponge
can desire, and, fortunately, by the time the Jawleyfords begin to
suspect that he has no money and begin to treat him badly as a consequence, Sponge receives that offer of "a better billet elsewhere,"
this one based on even more obviously false expectations. On his
first day's hunting with Lord Scamperdale, Sponge had failed to introduce himself and the rumor started that he was a great sporting
writer remaining incognito to evaluate better the hounds and the
field. To his credit it must be stated that Sponge is completely unaware of the false identity imposed on him, and when Mr. Puffington, master of the Hanby hounds, asks him to visit, Sponge has
no idea that the invitation is extended solely on account of Puffington's desire for publicity. So when life becomes intolerable at
Jawleyford Court, Sponge moves on to Hanby House and Mr. Puffington. Mr. Watson describes Puffington simply and accurately as
"a Waffles grown up and still in possession of a fortune,"[21] another
perfect victim and another conceited swell. Again Sponge eats and
drinks and hunts and stays, stays, stays. The nearly distracted Puffington is finally rescued from Sponge's company by an invitation
for the latter to visit the Jogglebury Crowdeys who, like the
Jawleyfords before them, think Sponge has a fortune. "The world is
generally very complacent with regard to strangers," writes Surtees,
"generally making them out to be a good deal better than they real-

ly are, and Mr. Sponge came in for his full share of stranger credit"
(371). "In short," sums up Mr. Noakes, "they were out to
'prospect' Sponge as if he was a goldmine."²² Here Sponge really
outstays his welcome. After a considerable length of time, the fat,
gibbey-stick-whittling Jogglebury becomes as desperate to be rid of
Sponge as his unfortunate predecessors had been.

True to his own plan of action, however, Sponge does not budge
until he is invited to stay with Mr. Facey Romford, a character to
whom Surtees was to return in his last novel, *Mr. Romford's
Hounds*, and for whom he lays the groundwork here. In Facey
Romford, Mr. Sponge encounters a man much like himself, and
Romford's is the only residence from which he removes of his own
accord. Romford lives in small rooms above a saddle shop, offers
Sponge a bed much too short for comfortable sleeping, plays his
flute terribly until Sponge is almost driven mad, and wins money
from him at *ecarte*. Sponge flees as if for his life to Nonsuch House,
an estate owned by Sir Harry Scattercash and inhabited by dozens
of disreputable hangers-on who, like Sir Harry, are constantly drunk
and irretrievably in debt. Here he manages to stay until the bailiffs
walk in and close the establishment.

Before that tragedy occurs, however, Soapey has an experience at
Nonsuch House unlike any he, or any other major Surtees character,
has ever known—he falls in love. One of the few invited guests on
the premises is "the beautiful and tolerably virtuous Miss Glitters,
of the Astley's Royal Amphitheatre, who had come to spend a few
days with her old friend, Lady Scattercash" (351). Lucy had started
her professional career as a rider in a circus, and when she hunts
with the party from Nonsuch House she and Sponge lead the field.
" '*Hold up!*' roared Mr. Sponge, as having bored a hole through the
fence, he found himself on the margin of the water-race. The horse
did hold up, and landed him—not without a scramble—on the far
side. 'Run him at it Lucy!' exclaimed Mr. Sponge . . . and Lucy,
fortunately hitting the gap, skimmed o'er the water like a swallow
on a summer's eve. 'Well done! *you're a trump!*' exclaimed Mr.
Sponge" (383). Lucy's beauty and pleasant disposition, capped by
her riding and hunting abilities, have their effect on hero Sponge.
"The fair lady leant towards him, and as he adjusted [the brush]
becomingly in her hat, looking at her bewitching eyes, her lovely
face, and feeling the sweet fragrance of her breath, a something
shot through Mr. Sponge's pull-devil, pull-baker coat, his corduroy
waistcoat, his Eureka shirt, Angola vest, and penetrated the very

cockles of his heart. He gave her such a series of smacking kisses as startled her horse and astonished a poacher who happened to be hid in the adjoining hedge. Sponge was never so happy in his life" (384). It should be pointed out that Lucy has no money nor any prospect of any money. "She was, in fact," says Watson, "exactly the kind of woman the professional sponge would never dream of considering. . . . Of all Surtees' characters . . . he alone accepted love without question or forethought."[23] With the fall of Nonsuch House Sponge marries Lucy, settles with her in London, and opens the Sponge Cigar and Betting Rooms in Jermyn Street, St. James.

" 'What a farce,' we fancy we hear some enterprising youngster exclaim,—'what a farce, to suppose that such a needy scamp as Mr. Sponge, who has been cheating everybody, has any money to lend, or to pay bets with if he loses!' Right, young gentleman, right; but not a bit greater farce than to suppose that any of the plausible money-lenders, or infallible 'tips' with whom you perhaps have had connection have any either, in case it's called for. Nay, bad as he is, we'll back old Soapey to be better than any of them,— with which encomium we most heartily bid him ADIEU" (408).

Soapey Sponge, after that first questionable incident with Waffles, becomes an endearing and memorable rascal. As was the case with Jorrocks in *Handley Cross*, he, too, has that quality which the reader must admire—the self-confidence that comes from knowing what one wants and knowing how to get it. He never takes advantage of anyone who can be hurt by his machinations; none of his victims really suffers more than minor inconvenience at his hands. "All that one can say about him is that once inside a house he preferred to remain," writes Frederick Watson. "He had the psychology of an inmate of a charity institution. There is no evidence that he drank, or swore, or borrowed money, or made love, either sacred or profane. He was, in fact, a very good sportsman, without much conscience, perhaps, in cash transactions, but perfectly straight-forward in his intention to hunt by hook or by crook."[24] Mr. Watson goes to great lengths to defend Sponge, even from the connotations of his name.

He was a cynic, not a sponge. To him the world was full of unworthy people who, as he knew from his wide experience, were actuated, like himself, solely by personal motives, and that it was his calling as a man of the world to turn these unchristian impulses to his own advantage rather than theirs. That is not sponging so much as survival of the fittest . . . he was a *man*,

not a toady, or a snob, or a whiner. He was also a worker, not a drone. The
activity of Sponge was that not of a social parasite, but of a horse-dealer; or,
to put it upon a purely business footing, he could not afford to hunt unless
he made it pay. Nothing could be more above board than that.[25]

Susan Hallgarth says it another way: "Although Sponge is a
rogue, he is a rogue with a difference, more natural and honest than
the traditional parasite who uses flattery, falsehood and intentional
hypocrisy to make his way in fashionable society."[26] Whatever his
motives, whatever justification, if indeed there is one, one applies to
his actions, no reader can remain detached from the world and
adventures of Soapey Sponge. The writing in this novel is at the
same time both more intense and more detailed than in *Handley
Cross*. Whether Soapey is dining or hunting, trading horses or
worrying about his next "billet," getting lost or falling in love, the
reader is sharing those experiences with him, experiences which he
will never quite forget.

But Soapey Sponge is just one of Surtees's masterfully drawn
characters in this novel; if anything, his minor figures here are more
colorful, more eccentric, and more finely produced than they were
even in *Handley Cross*, and most of them are humbugs of the first
order. To highlight this aspect of their characters and to contrast
them immediately to the unpretentious and therefore "good
fellow" Sponge, Surtees developed the style of introducing each
character with a few short lines of description that provide the
reader at a glance with both the physical appearance and psy-
chological deformities of the person. The result is that every
character fairly leaps full-blown into the reader's consciousness. Mr.
Benjamin Buckram, the London horse dealer who supplies Sponge's
horses, "though far from being one, had the advantage of looking
like a respectable man. There was a certain plump, well-fed rosiness
about him, which, aided by a bright-coloured dress, joined to a continual fumble in the pockets of his drab trousers, gave him the air of
a 'well-to-do-in-the-world' sort of man." His employees "were of a
very shady order. Dirty-shirted, sloggering, baggy-breeched,
slangey-gaitered fellows, with the word 'gin' indelibly imprinted on
their faces" (7 - 8). Mr. Caingey Thornton, a friend of Waffles who
has the honor of riding the infamous Hercules through a shop window, is "as big a little blackguard as any in the place—lives upon
Waffles, and yet never has a good word to say for him, no, nor for
any one else—and yet to 'ear the little devil a-talkin' to him, you'd

really fancy he believed there wasn't not never sich another man in
the world as Waffles—not another sich rider—not another sich
racket-player—not another sich pigeon-shooter—not another sich
fine chap altogether" (29).

No reader can forget Lord Scamperdale, "stumpy, and clumsy,
and ugly," a man who "came to the determination not to marry in a
hurry; and until he did, he felt there was no occasion for him to inconvenience himself by living" (130). Scamperdale is completely
devoid of pretension; although certainly eccentric, he is another
natural man—but with a difference. He has an alter-ego in the
character of look-alike Jack Spraggon, and while Scamperdale's
social position prohibits him from swearing, Jack more than makes
up for his master's loss of words. Between them, their ability to
swear and the size of their collective vocabulary and ingenuity in
the use of it fill the reader with envy. When Sponge is unable to
stop Hercules from running over the hounds, Scamperdale starts the
barrage of epithets. " 'Oh, you pestilential son of a pontry-maid!'
screeched his lordship, as Brilliant ran yelping away from under
Sponge's horse's feet. 'Sing out Jack! sing out!' " and he hands the
responsibility for continued swearing over to Spraggon, who picks it
up nicely. "Oh, you scandalous, hypocritical, rusty-booted, numb-
handed son of a puffing corn-cutter, why don't you turn your attention to feeding hens, cultivating cabbages, or making pantaloons for
small folk, instead of killing hounds in this whosesale way!"
Scamperdale picks up the reigns again, in a more refined manner as
befits his station. "Oh, you unsightly, sanctified, idolatrous,
Bagnigge-Wells coopersmith, you think because I'm a lord, and
can't swear or use coarse language, that you may do what you like;
rot you, sir, I'll present you with a testimonial! I'll settle a hundred
a-year upon you if you'll quit the country" (123). When a collision
with Sponge knocks Scamperdale off his horse, his repertoire ranges
from self-pity, "I'm kilt! He's broken my back,—he's broken my
legs,—he's broken my ribs,—he's broken my collar-bone,—he's
knocked my right eye into the heel of my left boot," to anger, "Oh!
will nobody catch him and kill him? Will nobody do for him?" to
the most damning curse he can lay tongue to, "Rot ye, Sir! hangin's
too good for ye! you should be condemned to hunt in Berwickshire
the rest of your life!" (181).

Old Tom Trowler, Waffles's huntsman, is captured in a
metaphor. "Old Tom, in his scarlet coat, black cap, and boots, and
Tom in his undress—say shirt-sleeves, shorts, grey stockings and

shoes, bore about the same resemblance to each other that a three-months dead jay nailed to a keeper's lodge bears to the bright-plumaged bird when flying about" (33). Three more sentences on Tom Trowler and Surtees has created a character that might have stepped straight out of a twentieth-century horror movie.

> On horse back, Tom was a cockey, wiry-looking, keen-eyed, grim-visaged, hard-bitten little fellow, sitting as though he and his horse were all one, while on foot he was the most shambling, scrambling, crooked-going crab that ever was seen. He was a complete mash of a man. He had been scalped by the branch of a tree, his nose knocked into a thing like a button by a kick of a horse, his teeth sent down his throat by a fall, his collar-bone fractured, his left leg broken and his right arm ditto, to say nothing of the damage to his ribs, fingers, and feet, and having had his face scarified like pork by repeated brushings through strong thorn fences (33).

Sir Harry Scattercast of Nonsuch House and his entourage are even more likely to make the reader shiver with disgust. "Sir Harry was a tall, wan, pale young man, with a strong tendency to *delirium tremens;* that, and consumption, appeared to be running a match for his person." On the day Sponge first hunts with them he finds that "Sir Harry and party had had a wet night of it, and were all more or less drunk. They had kept up the excitement with a champagne breakfast and various liqueurs, to say nothing of cigars. They were a sad debauched-looking set, some of them scarcely out of their teens, with pallid cheek, trembling hands, sunken eyes, and all the symptoms of premature decay." The tableau is completed with a touch of humor, "Lady Scattercash, with several elegantly-dressed females, all with cigars in their mouths" (298 - 299).

These are a few of the dozens of minor characters who appear in the story only briefly; people who are around for several chapters are so well drawn that the reader comes to consider them, in spite of their oddities and Surtees's obvious intent to make them unsavory for the sake of his satire, rather endearing friends. A primary example is poor, fat Mr. Jogglebury Crowdey, who has to be suffering from advanced emphysema. Every word he speaks is accompanied by gasps and wheezes. He is such a pleasant and harmless fellow with his pretty wife, twelve children, and house full of intricately carved walking sticks that the reader almost wishes he could be spared the irritation of Sponge. He is an interesting character in that he falls in that social spectrum much closer to the natural Romford and to Sponge himself than to the artificial Waffles, Puf-

fington, Jawleyford, or Scattercash. For this reason he is a more
sympathetic character, although his naiveté in inviting Sponge to
his home solely on the basis of the stranger's reputed wealth places
him squarely in the classification of gull. Even his introduction to
Sponge is agonizing. " 'I was going to say (hem—cough—hem),' at
length observed he, looking up; 'that's to say, I was thinking
(hem—wheeze—cough—hem), or rather I should say, Mrs.
Jogglebury Crowdey sent me to say—I mean to say,' continued he,
stamping one of his ponderous feet against the floor as if to force
out his words. 'Mrs. Jogglebury Crowdey and I would be
glad—happy, that's to say (hem)—if you would arrange (hem) to
(wheeze) pay us a visit (hem).' " What he will have to deal with as a
result of that unfortunate and ill-timed invitation is immediately
evident, for Sponge, anxious to leave Puffington's, replies, "Well,
you're a *devilish* good fellow! and I'll tell you what, as I'm sure you
mean what you say, I'll take you at your word and go at once." This
is certainly not what Jogglebury expected, especially since this is the
first time he has ever met the man, and he tries pathetically to undo
the damage he has done. " 'Oh, but (puff—wheeze—gasp),' started
Mr. Jogglebury, the blood rushing to his great yellow, whiskerless
cheeks, 'I'm not quite (gasp) sure that Mrs. (gasp) Jogglebury (puff)
Crowdey would be (puff—wheeze—gasp) prepared.' " The reader
momentarily hates Sponge for his insolent "Oh, *hang* preparation!
I'll take you as you are" response (268 - 269). Admittedly this is one
of the few times the reader's sympathy lies with Sponge's victim,
but it is, at least for the moment, so *completely* with Jogglebury
that again one must admire Surtees's ability to add interest and
variety to his writing by deliberately and cleverly manipulating his
reader's emotions.

It is ironic that Surtees, who was so well able to play on his
reader's feelings in this way, should be accused of having a lack of
emotion himself, for he was never one to spoil a scene with sentimentality. A good case in point is the death of Jack Spraggon at
the "Grand Aristocratic Steeple-Chase." This is the first time
Surtees has permitted such a tragedy in his novels, and it is true that
he passes it off with almost shocking casualness. Those who point to
this scene as symptomatic of the writer's heartlessness, however,
quite miss the point. Even Mr. Cooper's assertion that "the occasion
might have been more successful had not Mr. Spraggon been a
character whose passing it is impossible to regret"[27] is more apology
for the author's handling of the scene than it is explanation.

Surtees's whole point in bringing in the steeplechase at all, aside from the literary advantage of collecting all his characters on stage for one last bow before the novel closes, is to argue that steeplechasing as a sport is stupid and inhumane and serves only to destroy good horses and men to the monetary advantage of gamblers and thieves and the satiety of the bloodthirsty appetites of ignorant people. "The work was written to decry the steeple-chase, betting list system, and winds up with one of those sorry affairs," he explained to Lord Elcho when he wrote for permission to dedicate the book to him.[28] What better way to illustrate that point than to have a man die a horrible, grotesque death while the horses race madly on, the mob cheers, and the gamblers count their money? All that is left to do at the end of the race is to calculate the damages. Jack Spraggon is dead, and the fact that the sponsor of the chase is convicted of manslaughter is little consolation. As for the rest, "the minor casualties of those few butchering spasmodic moments . . . were more numerous than most sportsmen see out hunting in a lifetime. One horse broke his back, another was drowned, Multum-in-Parvo was cut all to pieces, his rider had two ribs and a thumb broken, while Farmer Slyfield's stack-yard was fired by some of the itinerant tribe, and all its uninsured contents destroyed" (405). There must have been little joy for Soapey Sponge in winning the race amid such devastation.

Surtees absolutely cannot be accused of heartlessness. If he were truly coldhearted, he would never have experienced or displayed such outrage at what he saw as a cruel, mercenary, bloodthirsty excuse for sport, and the fact that this particular incident received negative criticism in Surtees's day reveals not only a Victorian critical penchant for sentiment but also a significant facet of Surtees's writing as well. "It may be said Surtees' humor is of an exceptional kind," Mr. Cuming declares. "Genuine humor and pathos go hand in hand; but this was not the case with Surtees, and he is the only genuinely humorous writer of whom it can be said. He is not pathetic even when the occasion urges."[29] Ms. O'Neill sees Surtees's handling of Jack's death as proof not of heartlessness but rather of his fine control as a writer of comedy. "Almost any other writer would have made this melodramatic or else allowed it to be repulsive," she says. "One never recognizes the born comedian so clearly as on the border of a tragedy."[30]

Mr. Sponge's Sporting Tour was Surtees's first successful novel so far as criticism and sales were concerned, and well it deserved to be.

After the fumbling of *Hillingdon Hall* and *Hawbuck Grange* the author had at last found his voice, and the public responded appreciatively. There can be no doubt that his association with the great illustrator John Leech, which started with this novel, helped the book's sales, but the pictures alone cannot account for the novel's popularity. Surtees himself must have been satisfied with the work, for he dedicated it to Lord Elcho, the man who had replaced Ralph Lambton in the author's esteem. He also wrote to Leech that "we have clearly hit the nail on the head, and we may as well drive it right home."[31] There is nothing hesitant or unsure about Mr. *Sponge;* it combines the best elements of *Handley Cross*—clever characterization, fast pace, detailed scenes of country living and country sport—with more major characters and better-caricatured minor characters to hold the reader's interest, more structure than he had so far employed, and a more clearly defined and effectively developed satirical scheme than in any of his earlier novels. It is, in every sense, a fine book.

CHAPTER 4

Young Tom Hall *and the Fashionable Parodies*

I Young Tom Hall

THE single most important thing about *Young Tom Hall is* the fact that it was never completed. The circumstances surrounding Surtees's abandonment of the novel and its effect on his next two books reveal a great deal about the man himself and his method of writing.

One condition upon which Surtees vehemently insisted in connection with the publication of *all* his work, with the exception of that early piece of nonfiction, the *Horseman's Manual*, was complete and absolute anonymity. All speculation on the possible reasons for such an attitude comes down to one point—he evidently felt that the writing of fiction was somehow below a country gentleman, that writing for profit was not a fitting occupation for a man of his position. "Writing was no longer a mere elegant accomplishment," points out Mr. Darton, "but it was hardly yet a trade for gentlemen."[1] There has even been made the suggestion that he was afraid such a rogue as Soapey Sponge might reflect badly on his own character. But his feelings went deeper than that, for even as a hunting journalist, a *professional* writer, he published primarily under the pseudonyms of "Nim South" or "John Jorrocks" or "The Yorkshireman" and admits in his memoirs that "I wrote on other subjects over other signatures."[2] Throughout his career he made deliberate attempts to disguise his authorship. For example, the prefaces for the three-volume editions of both *Handley Cross* and *Hillingdon Hall* are dated "Hoddesdon." As Mr. Cuming explains, "There is nothing among Surtees' papers to suggest that he was ever in the little town, much less that he ever lived there; and it may be assumed that he adopted this address as a blind to further conceal his identity from the general public."[3] And when a reviewer for the *New York Spirit of the Times* guessed that Nimrod had created Jorrocks, Surtees slyly half agreed. "This is a suspicion of our own which is not sustained by the opinions of many gentlemen with whom we have conversed," he writes. "But, whoever may be the author, we like the Lectures, and would rather have written the second one than any number of Tours, so full is it of wit and pleasantry, such practical shrewdness and knowledge of the science of 'unting and 'osses."[4]

In light of these facts it seems probable that his passion to remain anonymous arose more from innate modesty than from feelings of guilt or shame. Surtees was a strong, self-confident man; he did not need that kind of publicity to bolster his ego or make himself important, and his satire demonstrates over and over again how much he hated people who flaunted their accomplishments to win public praise. In *Hawbuck Grange* he states his position clearly and emphatically. "We may say, with our excellent friend Peter Morris, that 'if putting our Christian name and surname at the beginning of a book were necessary conditions to the dignity of authorship we should never be one while we live.' Like Peter, 'we want nerves for this.' We rejoice in the privilege of writing and printing *incognito*, and think with him that it is the 'finest discovery' that ever was made."[5]

With such sincere and long-standing bias in favor of the protection of his literary privacy, it is no wonder Surtees reacted strongly to the violation of that privacy by a man whom he felt he could trust, the publisher William Harrison Ainsworth. "I find I can write much better and with far more pleasure to myself when I am free to deny authorship if I like,"[6] he explained in a letter to Ainsworth (but Mr. Cuming is quick to add that "In all his correspondence I have found no evidence that Surtees ever did repudiate authorship of anything he wrote"[7]). The publisher did respect Surtees's wishes all the time *Mr. Sponge's Sporting Tour* was running in installments in the *New Monthly*, and Surtees expected the same consideration to continue when the *New Monthly* began publishing *Young Tom Hall* in October 1851. But, as Mr. Cooper says, Ainsworth "was only biding his time." "He was not above making capital out of the name and social standing of his authors," Cooper continues. "He was anxious to use Surtees' name because it now carried some weight as the editor of the *New Sporting* and the author of several sporting novels, and also . . . because he was a country squire and had been a master of foxhounds."[8] Mr. Noakes states that in 1845 Ainsworth actually made an announcement that "under his management the periodical would publish the work of authors 'eminent not only for talent but for high rank."[9] So, in an evident attempt to slip it by Surtees, he ran an advertisement mentioning the author by name. "The matter of the advertisement could have been composed between two men of more accommodating temperament," guesses Cooper. "But neither of them would go an inch to meet the other, and an acrimonious correspondence put an end to a profitable association and to a personal friendship."[10] Surtees protested immediately. "I cannot permit the use you are making of my name and must request you will immediately withdraw it from the *New Monthly* advertisement" (358). Ainsworth later claimed to have been hurt by Surtees's brusque command, but considering his own response, he had no right to complain. "I beg to enclose cheque on Coutts and C. for £6 in payment for the present chapters of *Tom Hall*," he wrote Surtees, and then added, "I shall be glad if you will wind up the tale as soon as you conveniently can."[11] Whether Ainsworth had been guilty of a gross blunder or an act of downright dishonesty in running that advertisement, his vengeful response would seem to indicate a guilty conscience. "An expression of regret, and assurance that the advertisement with Surtees' name had been withdrawn—as actually was done—and the matter would have blown over," Cumings guesses. "A little more tact on Ainsworth's part, and we should have had a whole story."[12] As it was, Surtees had had enough, and he responded simply, "I beg to acknowledge the receipt of your note and cheque for the January portion of *Hall*, which it is not my intention to continue" (359).

The story had run to sixteen installments; Surtees never finished the novel. He couldn't bring himself to abandon it altogether though, and he tried to restore it in bits and pieces by using many of the same characters and incidents in his next two novels. Such patchwork is seldom successful, however, and in *Ask Mamma* and *Plain or Ringlets* it is extremely disappointing. *Tom Hall* was on its way to being one of Surtees's best novels; those two which succeeded it and were made up in part from it are among his worst.

Young Tom Hall is something of a departure for Surtees, for in it one sees him gradually drawing away from the hunting field and focusing his attention more and more on the nonhunting element of country society. His next two novels continue the trend and can be appropriately classified, as they are by Ms. Hallgarth, "fashionable parodies" as opposed to sporting fiction. The most noticeable difference between the two types of novels is the difference in their main characters, for rather than being true and enthusiastic sportsmen, these men use the hunting field merely to gain social advantage. In fact, of the four heroes in these three books, two of them, Tom Hall and Billy Pringle, genuinely hate to hunt, a third, Jack Bunting, knows virtually nothing about the sport in the beginning but gradually becomes initiated and enthusiastic before the end of the novel, and a fourth, Jasper Goldspink, never hunts at all! But there is more separating Surtees's natural from his artificial heroes than the hunting field. Susan Hallgarth explains the difference.

> He implies that his rogues, asocial beings who make their way by taking advantage of the artifice in social pretension, are good men because of their common sense, lack of pretension, free expression of emotion, and sincerity. Though they can adopt social artifice as a means to their own ends, these rogues are essentially disinterested in social status. They are natural men placed in an artificial world. His dandies, on the other hand, innocently attempt to emulate the external manners of the upper class in order to raise their social status, but they succeed only in becoming victims of a society that is composed of artifice. In any case, Surtees' world is the world of fashionable rural society, and by juxtaposing natural with artificial characters, he exposes the incongruity between its appearances and reality.[13]

Tom is an interesting leading character for Surtees—a young, somewhat slow-witted fat youth who, blind to his own size, thinks of himself as a great dandy and falls madly in love with every woman he meets, "a good-natured goose without the drawback of the Sponge rascality" (x), as Surtees describes him in a letter to Ainsworth. He is a social climber, but a rather uninspired one. He is perfectly happy lounging around the streets in his fancy clothes with his equally purposeless buddies; he gets involved with life (goes hunting, joins the army, buys horses) only because others, particularly his current heart-throb, Angelina, and her father, Colonel Blunt, either inveigle or trick or downright push him into it. He is the first of Surtees's characters who, like those in his next two novels, is more acted upon than acting. Tom's father, too, is instrumental, either directly by command or indirectly by influence, in shaping Tom's life. He is a most frugal and clever banker who has amassed a considerable fortune which will, of course, someday belong to Tom; he wants Tom to be a gentleman, and everyone else wants Tom's money. His impending fortune alone makes Tom popular—popular with the women who want to marry him for it and popular with the men who want to do him out of it. In the completed portion of the novel Tom has several encounters with both greedy types; in fact, such encounters constitute not only the entire action of the novel, but its entire satiric purpose as well. Instead of going out into the world as Jorrocks and Sponge and, to a lesser degree, Tom Scott did to adventure among satirical social types, Tom merely sits back and lets them come to him. He is to be "a victim instead of a shark," writes Surtees. "He is to be well cheated by the men and courted by the ladies, and desperately tumbled about out hunting" (x). Consequently, the number of characters in this novel is more limited but those that are presented are more fully developed, less obviously caricatured, than those in the earlier novels.

Foremost among the ladies who vie for Tom's attentions is the attractive and well-seasoned Miss Angelina Blunt, daughter of Colonel Blunt of the Heavysteed Dragoons. "She had all the worldly experience of a woman of thirty. She had flirted with and jilted half the young men during their passage through the regiment . . . courting as a soldier's daughter ought to court—by word of command—making up to this man when told he was a 'catch'—chopping over to that when advised he was 'better' " (32). Tom's romantic heart is no match for her accomplished coquetry and he suddenly finds himself proposing, thinking he is the luckiest man in the world. Angelina accepts, of course, referring to him as "Greasy Tom" and laughing at his fatness and foolishness behind his back, but perfectly willing to go along with the engagement and probably even the marriage if nothing better, that is, richer, comes along. Tom is completely blinded by her beauty and dominated by her superior experience and intelligence. Fortunately for him, however, he is extremely fickle, and by the end of the completed portion of the novel Surtees holds out some hope that Tom will throw Angelina over for Laura Guineafowle, his latest "crush." Ms. Hallgarth suggest that "both Tom and Angelina have anti-romantic roles that parody the affected sentiment of the fashionable novels."[14]

Angelina so obviously plays Tom for a fool that the reader wishes on her all kinds of bad fortune, and she does eventually pay the

price for her heartless greed in an affair to which critics point as indicative of Surtees's indifferent and even unfair treatment of
women. For in the course of her maneuvers with Tom she entices
him onto the hunting field, where her good looks and great riding
ability bring her to the attention of a wealthy old bachelor rogue
named Lord Heartycheer, ". . . a great patron of the fair sex,
among whom he enjoyed a great reputation. . . . There had been
as great a succession of favourites at the Castle as there had been of
sportsmen with his hounds." His lordship is "now well turned of
seventy" (86), still handsome, still charming, still rich, and still a
first-rate sportsman. He is, in fact, an able adversary for the
machinations of Angelina. One never really knows just how serious
Heartycheer is about the scheming Miss Blunt; what one does know
is that, as a result of the Lord's attentions, Angelina "would have
backed herself at ten to one to be a countess" (324). Heartycheer
arranges a quiet hunt with Angelina, an excuse, of course, for the
beginning of a romantic liaison. The hopes of both the seducer and
the nearly seduced are literally dampened, however, by a driving
rainstorm which catches them far from home. Angelina "began to
be nervous. Rain never improved any woman's looks" (330). But
since there is no help for it, she goes gamely on until she is "quite
spoiled. The lustre of the feathers was quite destroyed, and the dye
of the brown Gariabaldi began trickling down her face. Her hair,
too, became loose, and fell wildly about her ears; her pink and
white kerchief was soaked, while her late looming-out habit stuck to
her figure like a wet bathing-dress. Altogether she was regularly
drenched" (332). The effect on her gallant old beau is immediate,
and the relationship and all her expectations come to a sodden end.
"His lordship marked the sad change, and already his fervent ardour began to cool. . . . The romance of the thing was fairly
destroyed. The poetry of the feather, the sentiment of the hat, the
taste of the tie were utterly ruined; and in place of a bright-eyed,
sunny-looking, well set-up girl, the old peer saw nothing but a very
downcast, draggle-tailed looking Miss, who, ere long, would be very
like her mother. And he was almost glad that it was too dark for the
grooms and people to see the figure she was when she got back to
the castle" (332 - 334).

The chauvinism in the scene is obvious, and every intelligent
reader must be offended by it. It may be, as Aubrey Noakes
suggests, "typical of Surtees' satirical, unromantic outlook that their
little flirtation ends disastrously in a downpour of rain,"[15] but it is

also, says Cooper, "poor and conventional fun, the very stuff of contemporary Victorian humour."[16] Despite all that, however, the reader still might find the scene strangely satisfying—Angelina is such a terrible person that the reader enjoys seeing her brought down to the level to which she brings everyone else. After all, she is, herself, completely without compassion; one who treats others as objects may deserve to be treated as an object herself. It is only when one places this scene in the context of Surtees's overall inadequate presentation of women that the true significance of its chauvinism overrides the reader's fleeting sense of satisfaction.

Although Tom and Angelina, as the hero and heroine, are the novel's main characters, they are almost overshadowed by those colorful eccentrics, their fathers. Old Tom Hall bears the nickname "sivin and four's elivin" for good reason. "Figures, figures, figures! Old Hall's head ran upon nothing but figures. His mind seemed to be formed of three red-ink columns, up and down which his thoughts circulated in the shape of pounds, shillings, and pence. . . . He could not answer a common observation about the weather without doing a little mental arithmetic while he thought the thing over. 'Fine day, Mr. Hall,' farmer Barleymow would say, as he stamped along to the market. 'Sivin and four's elivin, and eighteen is thirty-nine. Yes sir, it *is* a fine day,' the banker would reply" (2). Surtees explains that "sivin and four must have stood Hall in good stead at some season or other in his life, for, to whatever length his calculations ran, he invariably commenced with 'Sivin and four's elivin,' and built up his column on that superstructure" (2). His mental calculations are truly extraordinary. When fat Colonel Blunt comes to call, Old Hall contemplates the colonel's blundering opening statement: "Sivin and four's elivin, and forty-nine's sixty (what a fat man he is), and sixty's a 'under'd and twenty, and ninety's two 'under'd and ten (I wonder whether he'll be asking me to do a bill), and twenty-nine's two 'under'd and thirty-nine (that's a piece of impittence callin' Tummus, James—knows his name's Tummus as well as I do), and forty-five's two 'under'd and ninety-four. . . ." (29).

Colonel Blunt is of a different order, a fat, loud, obscene "monster" of a man who at some time or other has cheated most of the men in his regiment and who uses his daughter in his deals just as readily as he uses his horses. In fact, when he first meets Tom, "having attentively scrutinized Tom's fat, vacant face, and considered whether he had better pigeon him or let his daughter have a

run at him, he came to the conclusion that he might do both" (10).
Mr. Cooper finds in him something to admire. "The triumphant
figure of the book is Colonel Blunt. . . . In his gross person and his
gauche manners he epitomizes all Surtees' hatred of the cavalry officer, yet there is something magnificent about him, something that
for a fleeting moment almost recalls Mr. Jorrocks. He was a rogue
and snob and a skin-flint where Mr. Jorrocks was none of them, but
he had about him something of the indestructibility, the resilience
that distinguished the Master of the Handley Cross Hounds. With
every turn of fortune and chance of fate against him, he refuses to
be quite subdued."[17] Mr. Johnston-Jones, on the other hand, finds
him thoroughly despicable. "One could indeed almost describe him
as insane, for he pays no attention whatsoever to anyone else's
thoughts or feelings and has quite lost the ability to see things from
any standpoint but his own: this sets him, as it were, outside
humanity. . . . Colonel Blunt at times becomes an almost horrify-
ing figure."[18] Again, one must marvel at the richness of Surtees's
characterization, for although Blunt seems to be one of the most exaggerated of Surtees's characters, he was evidently based on a real
person—Ainsworth wrote to the author, "I suppose you have old
T___in your eye."[19]

Not only Blunt, but the entire troop of Heavysteed Dragoons are
fine characters. "It is difficult to believe that any mess could be
quite so corrupt and dissolute," writes Cooper. "There is not an
honest or sober man among them. Individually they are beneath
contempt. Together they move through the book with a richly
collective humour that makes them irresistible."[20]

Young Tom Hall showed promise of becoming one of Surtees's
best works. "In a word," writes Mr. Cuming, "up to this stage it
seemed as though 'Tom Hall' was destined to enjoy a success as
great as 'Mr. Sponge."[21] Mr. Hamilton goes even further. "There
are," he says, "no voices dissenting from the argument that in
Young Tom Hall he was most of the way towards creating a novel
as good as Handley Cross."[22] In any case, this fragment of the novel
is fast-moving and genuinely interesting. The male characters are
all types new to Surtees, and he obviously enjoyed them. All his
characters here carry that distinguishing Surtees mark of individuality, of somehow being larger than life, more real than real
people. The novel abounds with jovial humor of the kind found in
the early Jorrocks books and in Mr. Sponge. His satire, although of
a slightly different focus, is good-natured and well-balanced

between standard Surtees sporting types such as Lord Heartycheer
and new satirical subjects such as old "sivin and four's elivin" Hall
and the Heavysteed Dragoons. Fat Tom himself demonstrates such
a balance within his own character, for he is "a transitional figure in
the development of Surtees' hero from the humorous, natural
picaros . . . to the artificial, stilted dandies of the fashionable
parodies. . . . Poor Tom is part gull and adventurer-social climber
and part mock-hero."[23] Whatever his literary ingredients might be,
Tom has one advantage that Surtees's next few heroes do not
have—he is a completely sympathetic character. As physically unattractive and slow-minded as he is, he is the one innocent, unam-
bitious person in the novel, and for that reason alone the reader is
entirely on his side.

Altogether, *Young Tom Hall* is a novel which the reader does not
like to see interrupted; he really wants to find out what happens to
Tom Hall and his engagement to Angelina and his new flirtation
with Laura Guineafowle and to Angelina's "second string," the little soldier called "Jug." He has not yet begun to tire of any of them.
Sincerely wishing to know how a novel ends is perhaps the highest
tribute a reader can pay to an author, but in this case he is doomed
to frustration, for the next two books, far from carrying on either the
story or the fun of *Young Tom Hall*, are very sorry affairs indeed.

II   Ask Mamma

Ask Mamma is an obvious offshoot from the preceding novel;
Lord Heartycheer reappears as Lord Ladythorne, still seventy years
old and still hunting both fox and young ladies; Dicky Thorndyke
becomes Dicky Boggledyke, huntsman to his Lordship in fields both
of sport and of romantic conquest; Major Guineafowle is Major
Yammerton, still hunting hare "five and twenty years without a
subscription"; Angelina Blunt reappears as the international coquette Miss de Glancey, who shares her predecessor's humiliating
drenching in the rain, a catastrophe which this time, of course,
quenches the ardor of Lord Ladythorne. Surtees "gave some of the
characters who figure in 'Tom Hall' a new lease on life," Cuming
explains. "To their creator they were real persons, and, their
possibilities not being exhausted on this stage, he brought them
forward on another under different names."[24]

Most interesting, however, are the similarities and differences
between the heroes of the two novels, for although Billy Pringle is

obviously based on Tom Hall, the two men appear to the reader as entirely different persons, and the novels succeed or fail to the extent that these characters capture the reader's interest and concern. Just as old Tom Hall balances his accounts and declares that "our Tom shall be a gent!"[25] so old William Pringle exclaims, "Our Billy shall be a gent!"[26] Old Hall's definition of a gentleman, "a man with plenty of money and nothing to do,"[27] applies as well to Billy as it does to Tom. Billy, just as much as Tom, lacks any self-motivation, any direction except that imposed on him by others. In fact, the only basic difference between the two characters is their size, for Billy Pringle is slender rather than fat, handsome in a pampered way rather than grotesque, and from that change in the physical appearance of the main character arises a vast difference in the reader's acceptance and interpretation of him. For instance, when Tom affects the "swell" he is completely ludicrous. No matter how showy his clothes or tight his new hunting boots, the reader always sees him as he is first introduced, "disporting himself on three chairs in the bay-windowed coffee-room of the Salutation Inn."[28] As a "round, fat, humming-top-shaped" man "upon whose plump limbs the flesh wobbled and trembled"[29] as he walks, Tom Hall is a perfect victim—the reader sympathizes with him because he has known and sympathized with fat people in real life. While it is true that the stereotype of the naive fat boy is offensive and even cruel, nevertheless it is this very stereotyping that saves Tom as a character, for the reader can accept him and even approve of him on the one-dimensional basis in which he is presented. But take away Tom's size and one has Billy Pringle, a very sad main character indeed.

While Tom is a reluctant social climber, his financial condition, parents, and friends urging the role upon him, Billy Pringle is a "swell" of the first order. Whereas Tom's actions, however absurd, have an air of naturalness about them, Billy is Paris-trained to play the snob. Another difference between them is that while Tom's money is real, Billy's is primarily a matter of reputation. Billy's entire character is a vast pretense, and the reader dislikes him immediately.

Considering that Billy Pringle, or Fine Billy, as his good-natured friends called him, was only an underbred chap, he was as good an imitation of a Swell as ever we saw. He had all the airy dreaminess of an hereditary highflyer, while his big talk and off-hand manner strengthened the delusion. It was only when you came to close quarters with him, and found that though he talked in pounds he acted in pence, and marked his fine dictionary words and laboured expletives, that you came to the conclusion that he was "painfully gentlemanly." . . . there was always a nervous twitching, and jerking, and feeling, as if he was wondering what people were thinking or saying of him (1 - 2).

Not only is he conceited, but he is dumb as well. It is interesting that while fat Tom's slowness seems somehow to pass for innocence, that same characteristic in slender Billy can be classified only as stupidity. His sole comment on any situation is a drawled "yarse." The reader cheers when Billy is sold an inferior horse by Major Yammerton simply because the reader likes Yammerton better than he does Billy. Such alienation of affection never occurs with Tom Hall. While Tom seems merely uninitiated, Billy appears bored and, considering his youth, strangely jaded. He has absolutely no control over his life nor any desire for such control. For instance, although he has never hunted, hardly ridden a horse, and is terrified of jumps, nevertheless he goes to the Earl of Ladythorne's for a week of fox-hunting because his mother thinks such a visit might provide him with social connections. He hardly makes a move unless he can first "Ask Mamma." She tells him by letter how to dress, what to say to the ladies, and even how to forward his own mail. She hires his groom and takes it upon herself to inquire into the details, particularly the financial ones, of the lives of everyone he meets. He can't be accused of having a simple mother-fixation, however, for he is equally pliable to the wishes of everyone he meets; he goes to Major Yammerton's because the major happens to invite him, and then to Sir Moses Mainchance's estate for the same reason. He drifts from place to place, from one detested hunting field to the next, always wondering, along with the reader, just what he is doing there. This is typical of one of the two types of classic picaros, however, as Susan Hallgarth describes them: there are "true picaros who are masters of their fate (the light-hearted Jorrocks and Tom Scott and the tough-minded Sponge and Romford); and feigned rogues who are actually fortune's butts (the dandified Tom Hall, Billy Pringle, Jasper Goldspink, and Admiration Jack Bunting)."[30] So little character does Billy have as a result that when his horse dies because of his neglect he does not even seem to care. And as far as Billy is concerned, the reader does not care either!

This sadly disappointing character Billy Pringle is symbolic of the inferiority of *Ask Mamma* to Surtees's earlier works, including *Young Tom Hall*. For one thing, the satire here has a different flavor. Watson calls it "bleak,"[31] Hallgarth says it has a "bitterness" of tone,[32] and Cooper states that the novel has "little geniality."[33] The new direction of Surtees's satire was already obvious in *Tom Hall*, but in that novel Surtees retains enough of his former successful character types and humorous situations to make a good novel. Here the satire is more limited, more clichéd, and often preachy. The primary difference, again, lies in the differences between main characters, for Tom Hall provides *Young Tom Hall* with a center of focus that *Ask Mamma* lacks. The reader cares about Tom, and this quality of caring raises him above the mere caricature, the butt of laughter, the pawn of satire. Although he is far from being a Jorrocks or a Sponge, he is sufficiently honest and natural to represent Surtees's satiric norm; he is the center of consciousness with which the reader identifies to watch and laugh at the absurdities around him. Such is not the case with Billy Pringle. If anything, Billy epitomizes everything Surtees could not stand, and, because he is allowed no redeeming characteristics, the reader cannot stand him either. Consequently he becomes the object of satire rather than the satirical norm, and the soul of the novel is gone; there is no chink in the satirical armor through which the reader can enter and view Surtees's world from inside. There is no John Jorrocks to laugh with, no Soapey Sponge to connive with, no Tom Hall to cheer for. The reader is kept emotionally outside the action while the *nouveau-riche* world of "swells" and hypocrites and social climbers·and jealous, possessive, self-satisfied, petty people, led by Billy Pringle himself, are paraded before him. The parade, from this distance, soon becomes obvious, repetitious, and dull. One gets the feeling that Surtees himself did not enjoy it anymore.

It would not be fair, however, to imply that the book has no redeeming qualities, for it has, and chief among them, as always, are some of Surtees's minor characters. Mrs. Pringle is a beautiful example of that character type Surtees most hated, the fortune-hunting, marriage-minded mamma. Having herself risen by a fortunate marriage from lady's-maid to comfortable mercantile middle-class, she is determined that her Billy shall use the same method to rise even higher. "Beware of Miss de Glancey," she writes her son. "*She hasn't a halfpenny*" (93). When Billy visits

Major Yammerton, with his three attractive, marriageable daughters, Mrs. Pringle is beside herself with worry. *"Beware of the girls!"* she warns. "There's nothing so dangerous as a young man staying in a country house with pretty girls. . . . *Be careful therefore what you are about"* (175). She is more than an over-protective mother watching out for the interests of her son—she is a virtual piranha. She evidently created quite an outrage when *Ask Mamma* first appeared, for even Mrs. Surtees felt obliged to come to her rescue, declaring she was "a far more respectable lady than Lucy Glitters."[34] Recognizing the Victorian concept of literary morality, one wonders if the objection to Mrs. Pringle might not have arisen from her happy ending, for at the conclusion of the novel she marries the Earl of Ladythorne. "Well done our fair friend of the frontispiece," applauds Surtees. "The pure white camillias are succeeded by a coronet! The borrowed velvet dress replaced by anything she likes to own. Who would have thought it!" (422). Not many, evidently, for the typical Victorian reader would not have considered this to be her "just" reward. Thus Mrs. Pringle stands as another example of Surtees's independent and un-conventional morality.

To speak of Surtees's morality makes it necessary to consider for a moment another character from this novel, Sir Moses Mainchance. Although he is another of those city-bred pseudo-country-gentle-men foreshadowed by Nosey Brown and Marmaduke Muleygrubs, he is different from them in one important way—important to Surtees, that is—he is "of Jewish origin." This makes him a new kind of character for Surtees, one that does not bring much credit to its creator. Sir Moses's family name had originally been Levy; his great-grandfather "dealt in complicated penknives, dog-collars, and street sponges. His grandfather, more ambitious, enlarged his sphere of action and embarked in the old-clothes line," to which he later added the sale of rhubarb and gum arabic. It was he who married a rich woman by the name of Smith, became a Christian, and dropped the Jewish name. Sir Moses's father carried on the family trades in addition to opening a "curiosity shop," a front, of course, for a loan business. It was as a result of his father's usury trade that Sir Moses acquired his title, for after his father's death he "was enabled through one of those monetary transactions to claim the services of a distinguished politician now no more, and obtain that hereditary rank which he so greatly adorns." His actions from that point on are predictable—"On becoming a baronet Sir Moses

Mainchance withdrew from commercial pursuits, and set up for a
gentleman, purchasing the magnificent estate of Pangburn Park, in
Hit-im and Hold-im shire, of which country he is a Deputy-
Lieutenant, getting together an unrivalled pack of fox-hounds"
(180). Sir Moses knows absolutely nothing about hunting or farming; he assumes that the hounds are necessary to his new image
and that his new estate will support him. He is, of course, wrong in
both assumptions, and the result, particularly of that second incorrect misconception, is disaster.

Sir Moses's property went rapidly back, and soon became a sort of last
refuge for the destitute, whither the ejected of all other estates congregated
prior to scattering their stock, on failing to get farms in more favoured
localities. As they never meant to pay, of course, they all offered high rents,
and then having got possession the Henerey Brown scene was enacted
—the farm was "far o'er dear"—they could "make nout on't at that rent!"
nor could they have made aught on them if they had had them for nothing,
seeing that their capital consisted solely of their intense stupidity. Then if
Sir Moses wouldn't reduce the rent, he might just do his "warst,"
meanwhile they pillaged the land both by day and by night (197).

It is obvious what Surtees was doing here; he was working into
his fictional novel the same ideas he would set forth three years later
in his unpublished article on Durham farming, the "Description of
Durham." In many places he even uses the same language. For instance, one can compare the following passage from the "Description" with the passage quoted above: "Leases, before the establishment of county courts, were of very little or no value in the county
of Durham. If the tenant had a good take, of course he stood by it;
if not, he treated the lease as so much waste paper. 'Aye, why, then
ye mun just de your warst,' they would say if the landlord
remonstrated. Meanwhile, of course, they did their warst with the
land."[35] As Mr. Cooper points out, "Every evil of small-holding
farmers which is touched on in the 'Description of Durham' is
represented on Sir Moses' estate."[36] In "Description," to take
another example, he talks about the tenants: "Under that pauper-
promoting system of allowing a running half-year, they think
nothing of facing the landlord at the end of a year with perhaps
only a quarter's rent in hand."[37] In *Ask Mamma* he writes: "And
now at the end of the year, (the farms being let on that beggerly
pauper-encouraging system of a running half-year) Henerey &
Humphrey came dragging their legs to the Park with a quarter of a

year's rent between them" (192). Between these two sources a great
deal can be learned about Surtees's agricultural ideas and his attitudes toward the current system and its victims.

All of this is very interesting, but what, one may ask, is it doing in
a novel? Surtees had never fallen back on lecturing before, not even
in *Hillingdon Hall*, his other novel dealing with agriculture. In fact,
even the political speeches in that earlier work, speeches obviously
serving as an excuse for Surtees to present his own opinions, make
better reading than this, for those speeches are delivered by John
Jorrocks who, while presenting the author's ideas, never steps out of
character. Here there is no spokesman—the digressions are spoken,
or rather preached, by Surtees himself. If they were to be lifted
from the novel and published separately they would constitute the
"Description of Durham"; as it is, they do nothing but slow the
book down.

And worse than that, these digressions sacrifice Sir Moses to their
didactic intent, for once his terrible failure as landlord is coupled
with Surtees's stereotype of the money-grubbing Jew, Sir Moses
becomes a despicable person and Surtees opens himself up to
charges of anti-Semitism.

It was Sir Moses Mainchance's misfortune to combine in his own person the
characteristics of all those classes of society whom Surtees most disliked. He
was a Jew, a dealer in horses, a pinching landlord, a would-be country
gentleman and a cheese-paring master of hounds. It is obvious that Surtees
disliked him more than any other character of his creation, and allowed him
hardly a redeeming feature. Sir Moses is no more unscrupulous in the
matter of horses than the Gentiles, Mr. Sponge and Mr. Romford, no more
offensive a parody of a country gentleman than Mr. Marmaduke
Muleygrubs. But where each of them excel in one particular department of
roguery or pretentiousness, Sir Moses excels in them all. And he is certainly
the worst land-lord in any of the books. It cannot be denied that his im-
perfection of all sorts sprang, in Surtees' opinion, from the common source
of his Jewish origin. He is almost the only character of them all to whom
Surtees makes no attempt to be fair and, coming from one so fundamental-
ly fair as Surtees was, it argues a depth of dislike beyond the ordinary.[38]

Mr. Noakes points out that this character is consistent in
demonstrating Surtees's agricultural views, for "in his opinion a
man needed to have a natural taste for rural life if he was to make a
success of farming and estate management. He was never tired of
attacking the paper-booted pen-and-ink landowners, with their

heads full of crackpot schemes, or those, like Sir Moses, interested both in setting themselves up as landed gentlemen and making money out of their land."[39] That point is certainly valid; Surtees goes so far as to say that "it may be laid down as an infallible rule that the man who has no taste for land or horses should have nothing to do with either. He should put his money in the funds"(100). But the author's deliberately making Sir Moses a Jew (one whose father had changed his name, as if trying to "pass") and making him greedy and cheating and a tightfisted screw besides would definitely seem to indicate more going on in Surtees's mind than he demonstrated with John Jorrocks in *Hillingdon Hall* or Marmaduke Muleygrubs in *Handley Cross*. Besides, when one adds to the characterization here the one other reference to Jews in Surtees's novels, one becomes even more justified in suspecting Surtees of prejudice. In *Plain or Ringlets* he introduces "Shadrac Absolam, the hook-nosed keeper of the Turkish Saloon and Oyster-rooms, who with a select party of cigar-smoking Israelites dashed past in a yellow barouche-and-four with dirty merry-Andrew-looking post-boys . . . and how complacently the Jews loll with their great arms over the sides, like half-drunken sailors on a spree"(81 - 82). But, whatever his prejudices might have been, in his usual style Surtees lets Sir Moses come out all right in the end, for he marries Clara Yammerton, and her father, a successful farmer knowledgeable in Surtees's favorite areas of draining and fertilizing, agrees to supervise Sir Moses's estate and rescues it and its owner from ruin.

This novel does have some more effective characters than the unfortunately stereotyped Mrs. Pringle and Sir Moses. For example, there is the inspired caricature of Cuddy Flintoff, one of what Surtees calls "mahogany hunters" because they do all their hunting in dinner-table conversation. Cuddy is "an 'all about' sportsman, who professed to be of all hunts but blindly went to none. Cuddy's sporting was in the past tense, indeed he seemed to exist altogether upon the recollections of the chase, which must have made a lively impression upon him, for he was continually interlarding his conversation with view holloas, yoicks wind 'ims! yoicks push 'im ups! Indeed, in walking about he seemed to help himself along with the aid of for-rards on! for-rards on! so that a person out of sight, but within hearing, would think he was hunting a pack of hounds"(215). Cuddy in action must have drawn a great number of wondering stares. "The joyful dressing bell rang, and Cuddy Flintoff putting his finger in his ear, as if to avoid deafening himself, shrieked, '*hoick holloa! hoick!*' in a tone that almost drowned the sound of the clapper. Then when the . . . footman appeared at the door with a blaze of bedroom candles, Cuddy suddenly turned whipper-in, and working his right arm as if he were cracking a whip, kept holloaing, '*get away hoick! get away hoick!*' until he drove Billy and Baronet and all before him"(216).

Unfortunately, a few truly clever characters and some genuinely funny scenes (Sir Moses springing his trap on his thieving housekeeper and her black-marketeering son as they drop a bundle of his household items from a second-story window—388 - 395; Jean Rougier / Jack Rogers, Billy's groom and valet, catching a fair Yammerton sister spy in "a *lee*-tle *contre-tems*"—117 - 120; Mrs. Yammerton serving a large number of important dinner guests on plates accidentally coated with castor oil—142 - 144) cannot redeem *Ask Mamma*. As a novel it is third-rate; compared to other Surtees novels the kindest word for it is dull. Part of the problem lies in the relentless satire which, without relief of any kind, soon renders itself boring. Another part of the problem lies with the reader's being forced to remain outside the action of the novel without a character with whom to identify, an enforced kind of objectivity that soon begins to cloy.

But the greatest part of the problem with this novel lies with Surtees—never before had he written with such hesitation, such insecurity. One can find whole chapters that add nothing whatever to the book: "The Major's Stud," "Cards for a Spread," "Commerce and Agriculture." On the occasion of Lord Ladythorne's hunt breakfast, the kind of scene in which Surtees usually excels, he deadens it with entirely too much detail; instead of highlighting the most interesting aspects, he describes *every* guest, *every* costume, *every* serving dish, *every* particle of food, *every* bit of conversation within the hearing of Billy or Ladythorne (61 - 70). Even the best-intentioned reader finds himself skimming and flipping pages.

Worse yet are Surtees's constant, irritating intrusions into the novel with tidbits of irrelevant information. One could make an extensive list of such things: "Posterity will know nothing of the misery their forefathers underwent in the travelling way" (9); "Some people can eat at any time, but to a well-regulated appetite, having to undergo even the semblance of an additional meal is inconvenient"(72); "A valet is absolutely indispensable for a young gentleman"(94); "no one ever goes into an inn in England that can

help it"(110); "How pleasant it would be if we were watched in all
the affairs of life as we are in eating"(113); "a good, hot well-
washed china dish is a great deal better than a dull, luke-warm,
hand-rubbed silver one"(114); "light wines and London clubs have
about vanished inebriety from anything like good society"(115 -
116); "No man thinks the worse of a woman for being able to
manage her house, while few men can afford to marry mere music-
stools and embroidery frames"(96); "Let any man of forty look at
his tailor's bill when he was twenty, and see what a liberality of innocence it displays"(146) and so on and on and on. Surtees had
already experimented with this technique with some success in
Hillingdon Hall and none at all in *Hawbuck Grange;* here it gets
entirely out of control. Susan Hallgarth explains what Surtees may
have been attempting to do. "Having chosen an inarticulate hero
who thinks 'of nothing but himself,' " she says, "Surtees is very
much a part of *Ask Mamma* as a commentator and master-of-
ceremonies combined. . . . Billy is so vague and idle that, were it
not for Surtees pulling the strings, his puppet would be completely
immobile; and since Billy has neither verbal nor visual reactions,
Surtees holds his own dialogue with the reader."[40]

Some of this dialogue, unfortunately, is actually offensive. For example, Surtees himself must have suspected early that his chapter
on "The Major's Stud" was not going well, but instead of changing
it or, better yet, eliminating it altogether, he tries to redeem it by
being clever. "Perhaps our sporting readers would like to take a
look into the Major's stable before he comes with his victim, Fine
Billy. If so, let them accompany us; meanwhile our lady friends can
skip the chapter if they do not like to read about horses—or here; if
they will step this way, and here comes the Dairymaid, they can
look at the cows. . . . Ah, we thought they would tickle your fancy"(121).

The novel does not "tickle the fancy" of the reader, however, and
the novel's new technique is not successful. It is impossible to ascer-
tain for sure just what happened to Surtees in this novel and his
next one, although most critics put the blame for their lack of
success on the interruption of *Young Tom Hall.* There Surtees had a
fine novel underway; when he was abruptly forced to abandon it,
he floundered. If he could have brought himself to finish it, even
with its greatly reduced chance of publication, he might have avoided this inspirational hiatus. As it was, instead of waiting for a new
idea, he grabbed at what he had—a character here, a scene

there—and tried to lump them together into some kind of whole, losing sight in the process of both his satirical direction and his reader. The effort was fruitless. Not only does the novel fail, but so does something else—Surtees's heretofore excellent critical judgment, for he plunged immediately into another such novel, salvaging what he could of the rest of *Young Tom Hall*.

III   Plain or Ringlets

Plain or Ringlets is unique among Surtees's works for one reason—of the three main characters, characters who among them provide the novel's points-of-view, one is a woman, Miss Rosa McDermott of Privett Grove. While it is true that in other works Surtees may present a woman in an important role, Mrs. Flather in *Hillingdon Hall*, for example, or Lucy Glitters Sponge in *Mr. Romford's Hounds*, such women are still completely dominated in literary terms by the novels' heroes, John Jorrocks and Facey Romford. Such is not the case in *Plain or Ringlets*, where Rosa plays an equal part with Jasper Goldspink and Jack Bunting, the other two corners of the love-triangle. None of the three is a pleasing character; in fact, to characterize their relationship as a "love-triangle" is misleading, for the only real love they are capable of feeling is for themselves or for someone else's money. Rosa speaks for all three when, warned by her lawyer not to marry hastily, she laughs, "Oh, you needn't be afraid of me, Mr. Ballivant! You needn't be afraid of me, I'm not one of the sentimental sort."[41] This novel, like its predecessor, is constructed of bits and pieces of *Young Tom Hall* carelessly thrown together with picnics and regattas and races and grand balls, "amateurish cobbling,"[42] as Leonard Cooper calls it. Here Surtees moves even farther from the sporting toward the social novel, for all the interest here centers around the marriage market, around the question of who will end up married to whom. Again Surtees makes the mistake of presenting no sympathetic character, no satirical norm against which to measure the absurdities of the rest of society. In fact, his main characters here are perfect examples of those kinds of people whom Surtees himself most disliked. Mr. Cooper is correct in his opinion that "in the matter of tedium there is little to choose between her two suitors, or in fact between them and Miss Rosa herself."[43]

"Admiration" Jack Bunting, "as he was commonly called, from his extreme satisfaction with himself," is one of Rosa's two beaus.

He is a great hoax, for "though he had the reputation of an immense fortune," he "had in reality nothing of the sort." What he
does have is some land in Scotland covered with unhealthy, stunted
trees, and a small building he refers to as his "castle." Surtees takes
pains to explain that "still there *was* the estate, and there *was* the
house, and, as the Judges lay it down every assizes, that 'a man's
home is his castle,' surely our friend had a right to call his shooting-
box a castle, if he liked." "He was young, gay, and good-looking,"
and like Tom Hall before him, he had "a great taste for beauty, and
abundant leisure to fall in love." He "had now run the gauntlet of
many fair maids, including a brunette or two, from whose
successive negations he always felt morally certain he could never
recover; yet somehow or other, after the lapse of a certain time, he
always found himself in just the same predicament with some other
young lady"(17 - 19). His numerous courtships frequently reached
the proposal stage, but a little investigation on the part of the intended's family lawyer soon uncovered his deceptions and he was
rejected, left to begin his seductions all over again. He follows the
lovely Rosa from the resort area of Roseberry Rocks to her home at
Privett Grove where he manages still another proposal and is again
rejected on the basis of the nonexistence of his supposed estate.
"Not that I advocate mercenary matches," insists the McDermotts'
lawyer, "but every day's experience shows one the necessity of
prudence and caution"(391). Nonsentimental Rosa agrees. "Jack is
an un-attractive creature," states Cooper. "There is nothing
definite about him. He has all Tom Scott's nebulosity without his
simplicity and modesty. In fact he is neither one thing nor the
other—neither wholly rogue like Sponge and Romford, nor fool like
Hall and Pringle, nor honest man like Jorrocks and Scott. He
meanders through the book, admiring his waistcoats and his
whiskers, and at the end we hardly know and certainly do not care
whether he has his castle and finds his heiress or not."[44] The only
encouraging sign which Jack displays is his newly acquired
enthusiasm for hunting. This alone is not enough to redeem his
dandified character, but it does make him more interesting than the
other two people who move through the book unchanged. In spite
of Cooper's statement of absolute indifference toward Jack, most
readers are probably not unhappy to discover at the end of the
novel that there are rich minerals under those straggly trees, and
that Jack will be a rich man.

Jasper Goldspink is the other "string" to Rosa's "bow." He more closely resembles Tom Hall in that he is a banker's son, his father being a reincarnation of old "sivin and four's elivin" Hall, and he is fat. Like Tom he is gullible and falls victim to the gambler O'Dicey just as Tom does to Colonel Blunt. But he is not developed as well as Tom—in fact, he is not developed as well as either Jack or Rosa. He is defined not as an individual but only in terms of his relationship to the other two, as Jack's rival and Rosa's "second string." Consequently the reader never really sees him clearly and cannot, of course, feel much for him one way or another. In the end Jasper does marry Rosa, not on his own merits but only because, after Jack is eliminated from the race, Jasper is the only man running. His final fate is just the opposite of Jack's, for a run on his father's bank leaves him and his new bride with nothing but each other for consolation—and well do they deserve each other!

Between these two "heroes" vascillates pretty Rosa, now wearing her hair plain to please Jack, now putting it into ringlets to please Jasper. It is between "plain" or "ringlets" that she must choose, and that choice is clearly to be made solely on the basis of monetary considerations. She cares nothing about the two men as human beings; she would just as soon marry fat Jasper as dandified, poetry-writing Jack if his financial status happens to be more favorable. She plays them off against each other in a truly heartless manner, turning their jealousy of one another into a weapon to bring them to terms. Although she is more fully developed than her predecessors, she is still a stereotype, another Emma Flather, Angelina Blunt, Miss de Glancey. The only thing that saves her from being completely contemptible is that she is no worse than her victims, for one can hate Rosa only so far as one pities them. When she ends up with only fat Jasper himself and no fortune, she deserves her "reward."

Leonard Cooper sees Surtees experimenting in *Plain or Ringlets* in two ways: first, "he seems to have realized the lack of feminine interest in his novels and to have determined this time to supply it at any cost to himself or his readers"; and second, "he seems, too, to have resolved to write a book without any hunting in it."[45] As far as the first point is concerned, if it is true that Surtees expected this novel to capture feminine interest, then he must have thought of his women readers as he did his women characters, as superficial beings interested only in marriage (not men, but marriage, an important distinction) and clothes. He states here that "women are educated now solely for the ornamental"(391), an ambiguous statement, for it is impossible to tell even in context whether he meant that women studied only "ornamental" crafts or whether he meant that women were educated to be mere "ornaments." Either way he was wrong; if Cooper's charge has any validity, then Surtees was evidently unaware that his countrywomen were fascinated by the complexity of Catherine Earnshaw and Jane Eyre, intrigued by the psychology of the female characters of Scott and Austen, and that they spent their spare time reading Byron and Keats. Those who would have been interested in reading anything, even the novels of Robert Smith Surtees, were definitely not Rosa McDermotts. As for Cooper's second charge, Surtees's avoidance of hunting, the author himself must have sensed that he was on the wrong track for after writing forty-one "tedious and silly"[46] chapters of "entirely fresh material, but of a quality and a sort which we have not yet met in Surtees, and happily never meet again,"[47] he introduces Jock Haggish and his hounds and, in his own special style, fills the last two-thirds of the novel with hunting scenes and sporting "characters."

As was the case with Sir Moses Mainchance and Cuddy Flintoff in *Ask Mamma*, the most interesting characters in *Plain or Ringlets* are those original to this novel, not carried over from *Young Tom Hall*. Mr. Jovey Jessop is one of Surtees's few successful "good" characters, another "golden thread" for his fabric, a "thorough sportsman, and a hearty hospitable man"(241). He is a bachelor with a large fortune who entertains a number of guests, many self-invited, to a fine dinner each evening, and who loans good horses to strangers like Jack Bunting when their own mounts fail them. His only problem is his inability to drink, a problem which he solves by keeping Thomas Boyston around as his "jug" to "carry away the wine in he couldn't hold himself"(246). Jug Boyston is a pleasing fellow to read about but not one whom the reader would choose as a friend. Not only does he take advantage of Jessop's hospitality, but he has a Soapey Sponge ability to get himself into other people's houses and to eat and drink his fill before he will suffer himself to be pushed out again.

Other interesting characters not original in type with this novel but not descending directly from *Young Tom Hall* are the Duke of Tergiversation and his wife, and Prince Pirouetteza. The duke had appeared briefly in *Hawbuck Grange* when his Fast-and-Loose Castle was the scene of a hunt which Tom Scott visited. Now he is fully drawn as one of Surtees's typical aristocrats, selfish and self-centered in the extreme. For example, he is always late, believing that there is "nothing like making people wait for giving them a due sense of one's importance"(274). He arranges his *battue* and grand ball "upon a sort of debtor and creditor principle, those from whom they expected to get anything being sure to be asked, while those who had been used were postponed for further consideration".(369). Worse yet, in Surtees's opinion, he uses the hunting field and his own pack of hounds solely for his social and especially political advantage. For the sport of hunting he has no affection whatsoever. He is "a munificent supporter of the chase in everything except the main essentials, viz., hounds, horses, and men. So far as dressing up in an orange-coloured coat, with cherry-coloured linings, collar and cuffs, with a white vest and white kerseymeres, to attend a hunt dinner or ball of an evening, his Grace was quite exceptional; but his exit from the smart Queen's-coloured barouche, with the four grays and postilions at the cover side, savoured more of the foot lights of the theatre than of the appropriate fitness of things so peculiar to fox-hunting"(146 - 147). The duchess is much like her husband, for she "used her country acquaintances merely as auxiliary to her London ones, sending for them when it suited her to have them, and snubbing them when it did not"(148).

Prince Pirouetteza is another of Surtees's terribly unfair portraits of foreigners, this one the last incarnation of his friend Baron Gablenz of Saxony and Brighton. He does not do Gablenz justice, however, for he was a true Baron whereas the Prince is the son of a dancing master at Florence. "Indeed he would have made a fortune if he had followed the paternal profession, for he was a natural dancer . . . but being just in the morning of life, with a little money left him by an uncle, he thought it would be far better to dance on terms of equality, and take whatever good the gods might provide. So he dubbed himself a Prince, and proceeded to enact the part"(181). Nor is he fair to Gablenz in the hunting line, for the Baron was an ardent hunter and a daring rider, while Pirouetteza can not tell a terrior from a hound, can not understand why it should take so many people and so many dogs to kill a fox when he did it very easily at the *battue* with one gun shot, and pleads minutes after the hunt starts that "I have had foxing enof . . . let me go ome to my music" (285). Pirouetteza is more than an unkind caricature of his Gablenz original; "he is the embodiment of those days at Boulogne . . . and of what the young Surtees remarked there, the foreigners' entire lack of perception of the importance of sport."[48]

Although *Plain or Ringlets* is not a successful novel, it is, however, an extremely important source of social history and of information about the ideas and feelings of Surtees. Instead of those irritating one and two sentence digressions that permeated *Ask Mamma*, in this novel Surtees devotes entire chapters to discussing various aspects of Victorian life, frequently comparing what he sees around him with conditions he knew as a young man. "It is appropriate that he should have dedicated it to his son," points out Mr. Noakes, "since the book embodies the reminiscent comments on life of a man in his early fifties and continual reference back from the present to the world of his youth—just the sort of comments one might expect from a man chatting with his son by the fireside."[49] He talks about the changes brought about by the railroad, changes affecting the lives of country squires. He talks about their new life-styles, about family servants and London clubs, about port wine and women's fashions, about newspapers and champagne. His depiction of daily life in resorts such as Roseberry Rocks with its promenades and gossips, its social-climbing and match-making, its utterly bored inhabitants trying desperately to have a good time, is fascinating in its attention to detail. He condemns horse-racing for its crookedness and the low class of people it attracts, but at the same time he suggests that public places of entertainment and instruction such as museums be opened to the public on Sunday, a revolutionary idea in 1860.

It is the work not of an old man, but of a man past his prime, whose thoughts are turning back to his early days and who is beginning to strike a balance between the good and evil that he has seen in his life. Such an account is of great interest for the record of the changes seen in forty years of an active life, but of still greater interest for the light which it throws on the accountant himself. . . . Surtees' world, it must be admitted, was a small and enclosed one, but he knew it perfectly. It is not until, as in *Plain or Ringlets* he leaves it for a while and gazes at the larger world, that we realize how enclosed it was. For his larger world does not extend very far beyond the wall of the country gentleman's park, nor does he stray very far from the railway line that leads from the counties to London. Uneven as the book is, it has its value for that picture of the Victorian world and still more for the picture of the man who looks at it. For once he has left the hunting field and walked abroad. "And no man," says the late Sir Walter Raleigh, "walks abroad save on his own shadow."[50]

"The fashionable parodies are the least successful of Surtees' novels," summarizes Ms. Hallgarth. "Their characters are less attractive and their tone more cynical and bitter; the satire seems diffuse, as though it were being directed toward life in general. Nor does Surtees appear to have been comfortable with his form or material. He interrupts twice as frequently in the parodies as he does in the picaresque novels . . . but is never quite able to instill his parodies with the gusto of the hunting novels or to impose the necessary unity on their multiple contrasts of social types."[51] Fortunately Surtees rediscovered his former direction, for with his last novel he turned for inspiration to the highly successful *Mr. Sponge.*

CHAPTER 5

Mr. Romford's Hounds:
Mr. Sponge *Resumed*

M R. *Romford's Hounds* is intended to be a sequel to *Mr.*
Sponge's Sporting Tour; consequently, many of the same
characters appear in both books; Facey Romford, Soapey Sponge,
Lucy Glitters, Jogglebury Crowdey, even Mrs. Scattercash. Facey
Romford is a character much like Soapey Sponge, a man of no personal means who lives by his wits—and lives well—much to the
detriment of other people. It seems as if, after the misfortune of
Tom Hall, Surtees was a bit unsure of himself; he wandered from
the hunting field into society, from natural men to "swells," from
chasing hounds to trapping mates. Now, twelve years after *Mr.*
Sponge, Surtees returned to that world of hunting field and country
gentlemen, leaving picnics, regattas, and most of the flirtation
behind. It was a truly inspired move, for it produced, as Cooper
describes it, "a straightforward sporting novel, a hunting comedy as
lively, as amusing and as competent as anything he ever wrote."[1]

Romford first made his appearance in *Mr. Sponge* when, caught
poaching on Jogglebury Crowdey's land by Sponge, he invited that
gentleman to stay with him. "Charlie Romford, or Facey, as he was
commonly called, from his being the admitted most impudent man
in the country, was a great, round-faced, coarse-featured, prize-
fighting sort of fellow, who lived chiefly by his wits, which he exer-
cised in all the legitimate lines of industry—poaching, betting, box-
ing, horse-dealing, cards, quoits—anything that came uppermost.
That he was a man of enterprise we need hardly add, when he had
formed a scheme for doing our Sponge."[2] His original intention was
to sell Soapey a bad horse, to outplay him at his own game as it
were, but he never had the opportunity, for by first winning "sivin
pun ten" from Sponge at cards and then actually having the audaci-
ty to demand an IOU, Romford revealed too much of his con-artist
temperament and his intended victim bolted. Nothing more was

seen of Facey Romford in that novel except for a brief appearance at the "Grand Artisocratic Steeple-Chase," where he came "to look after that sivin pun ten."[3]

In *Mr. Romford's Hounds* Facey moves forward to play the starring role. Already the reader has an advantage over Facey, for he knows from *Mr. Sponge* that Romford's beloved "Oncle Gilroy," to whom he had "early in life voted himself heir" and determined to "just hang about until his uncle was done with his shoes, and then be lord of Queercove Hill," actually "had a left-handed wife and promising family in the sylvan retirement of St. John's Wood." Poor Romford never suspects the existence of closer heirs to the family fortune, and the result is a good many lost years while Gilroy "just encouraged Facey in his shooting, fishing, and idle propensities generally, doubtless finding it more convenient to have his fish and game for nothing than to pay for them."[4] *Mr. Romford's Hounds* opens with Facey, upon Uncle Gilroy's death, discovering the disastrous truth. He is virtually overcome by panic. "Oh, Francis Gilroy Romford, moy beloved friend, you are regularly floored—done brown! That wretched old Oncle has sold you! Oh, Francis Gilroy Romford, discard the detested name of Gilroy, and be forever after Romford only. Oh, Francis Romford, Francis Romford, what are you now to do—what are you now to do?"[5]

At the time the aforesaid calamity befell him, he was just turned of thirty-one, tall and muscular, with a broad expansive chest, heavy round shoulders, and rather knock knees. His large backward-growing-all-round-the-chin-gingery-whiskered face was lit up with a pair of little roving red-lidded pig eyes, that were constantly on the watch—sideways, lengthways, cornerways, all ways save frontways. He looked as if he was always premeditating a parable, but somehow never produced it. Not that he was a fool—far from it, as those who had had anything to do with him in the betting or horse-dealing lines could testify; but he looked like a satirist who could cut a man in two with sarcasm, only, like a generous giant, he refrained from doing so. In short, a sort of you'd-better-leave-me-alone-looking man (7 - 8).

Perhaps the best description of Facey's physical appearance is that which occurs to the mind of Miss Anna Maria Hazen, who "looked deliberately at him, and thought what a queer-looking man he was,—queer eyes, queer nose, queer hair, queer altogether. 'Must be rich,' thought she, 'he's so ugly' "(228). Fortunately he is a man whose courage and ingenuity match his formidable appearance, for he is not one to be kept down long, not even by sneaky Uncle Gilroy.

His first step is to set himself up with a little capital, and to that end he borrows money from his old friend, Mr. Jogglebury Crowdey, the fat, wheezing, gibbey-stick maker from *Mr. Sponge,* to finance a trip to London supposedly to see to his Uncle's affairs but really to collect that debt of "sivin pun ten" owed him by Sponge.

A great deal has happened to Soapey Sponge and his bride, the lovely former actress Lucy Glitters, since the end of *Mr. Sponge's Sporting Tour* which left them proud owners of the new Sponge Cigar and Betting Rooms, "a happy combination, that promised extremely well at the outset, but an unfeeling legislature, regardless of vested interests, had presently interposed, and put a stop to the betting department"(15). With that calamity the Sponges were reduced to income from the tobacco shop alone, and although Lucy minded the store diligently, "still Soapey and she could not make both ends meet; and when poverty comes in at the door, love will fly out of even a glittering cigar-shop window"(15). Sponge began to gamble, to stay out all night, to drink too much. This is the situation when Facey Romford tracks them down in Jermyn Street.

Some good fortune is still on the side of Sponge, however, for happening to look through a peephole from the back room he sees Romford enter his shop and manages to avoid him for several days until finally, in a manner totally unbefitting the Soapey Sponge of *Mr. Sponge's Sporting Tour,* he suddenly disappears, leaving his debts, his shop, his Lucy, and the bothersome Mr. Romford behind. Facey, giving up for the time being the prospect of getting his "sivin pun ten," casts about for a new career. He decides to become a Master of Fox-Hounds.

There is one more detail of Facey's life that is of utmost importance to him—that is the strange and lucky coincidence of the existence of another, rich, Francis Romford. As Surtees explains,

It was lucky for our friend Mr. Romford . . . that there was another Mr. Romford in the world of much the same tastes and pursuits as himself, for our Mr. Romford profited very considerably by the other Mr. Romford's name and reputation. In the first place they were both called Frank, and in the second place they both kept hounds . . . and the mere fact of their doing so was very confusing. Added to this, our friend Facey being of the pushing, acquisitive order, accepted the change without doubt or hesitation. We don't mean to insinuate that he went about saying "I am the rich

Mr. Romford, owner of Abbeyfield Park, patron of three livings, J.P., D.L.," and all that sort of thing; but if he found he was taken for that Mr. Romford, he never cared to contradict the impression. Indeed, if pressed, he would mount the high horse and talk patronisingly of the other Mr. Romford—say he was a deuced good fellow, if not much of a sportsman, and altogether pooh-pooh him considerably. To hear Facey talk, one would think that he had not only persuaded himself that he was the right Romford, but had made the right Romford believe so too (1 - 2).

To forward his career as master of hounds Facey makes promiscuous use of the "real" Mr. Romford's seal, "a Turbot sitting upon its tail on a cap of Dignity," by attaching it to all his correspondence. It is not long before he has an offer—the gentlemen of the old-established Heavyside Hunt are in need of a master, and since they "thought they were communicating with the other Mr. Romford, who if they could but get to adopt their country, it would save them all further trouble about subscribing . . . indeed, Mr. Romford was known to be very rich" (23), they offer Facey the position for £800 a year. Trading on the Romford name, with generous use of the "Turbot sitting upon its tail," Facey equips himself with the horses and accoutrements necessary to his new image and sets off to take the pack at Minshull Vernon.

Fortunately for Facey he happens to be an excellent sportsman and becomes an excellent master of hounds. "Whatever the pack or country, whatever the horse he was hunting," writes Mr. Watson, "the most superior must have felt quite sure that Facey could be relied upon to kill foxes. . . . There are three essentials for the higher rank of huntsman. He must be with his hounds, which may mean . . . some heartbreaking falls, he must have the sense to leave them alone at a check, and after, if they fail to pick up the line, he must have an instinct . . . which tells him the direction the fox has taken. Only one huntsman in a hundred exhibits these three accomplishments," Watson continues, "But Facey did, and in consequence he remains the most naturally gifted huntsman in Surtees' or any other novels."[6]

Despite his considerable ability, however, Romford's reign with the Heavyside Hunt is short-lived. At first he is extremely popular; "he rose rapidly in public estimation, and his fame kept increasing every time he went out" (51). His mistake is in letting his horse-dealing get in the way of maintaining his popularity. On a quick trip to London he picks up a beautiful cream-colored horse named Leotard who at times "would do exactly what he was wanted; at other times he seemed to be possessed of a devil, and would do nothing but either run away or rear" (58). To prove to his constituency that the horse is not vicious, especially after Leotard sets Mrs. Rounding down in a mud puddle, Romford invites Lucy Glitters Sponge to Minshull Vernon to show the doubting natives how well Leotard behaves with a competent horsewoman. There can be no question that he has been favorably struck by Lucy's appearance ("slightly advanced in *embonpoint* since we saw her, but still in the full bloom of womanly beauty"—16) and demeanor during all those hours he observed her behind the cigar store counter, and besides, he is well aware that Lucy's early circus training and her hunting experience enable her to ride any horse and outride almost any man. "Lucy jumped at the offer, for she was well-nigh suffocated with fog and bad air, and felt that a run in the country would do her an infinity of good" (70).

This invitation to Lucy proves to be a mistake; her very first appearance with the Heavyside Hunt, when she rides as whipper-in for Facey, precipitates a crisis. The men are shocked and their wives outraged. They were already suspicious of Facey because of his horse dealings, and now they think he has gone too far. The wives, especially, have had enough: "They talked, and fumed, and stimulated each other into a grand phalanx of resistance. 'No pretty horse-breaker!' was the cry" (83). They control the ultimate weapon, their husbands' appearance at or disappearance from the hunting field, and they use it; before long Facey and Lucy find themselves riding alone. "Then Mr. Romford, finding himself in a fix, dislodging the Turbot for a time, mounted his cap of dignity, and resolved, if he was to lose the country, to sell himself as dearly as he could" (84). So he pockets the subscriptions, having now more money than he has ever had in his life, and taking his horses, his hounds, and Lucy, he heads for his next position as master of hounds of the Larkspur Hunt in Doubleimupshire.

Knowing that his stay in Doubleimupshire may also be of short duration since any stray sportsman from Minshull Vernon or any tourist from the Queercove Hill neighborhood or from London might recognize him and reveal him as the "wrong" Romford, Facey and Lucy set out, as Lucy says, "making hay while the sun shone" (240). Their first good fortune is to rent beautiful Beldon Hall from its nervous owner, Lord Lovetin, now on an extended visit to the continent, who feels safe in the rental only because he had known the other, the "real" Mr. Romford, at Eton. Their next problem is to invent a plausible identity for Lucy, who obviously can't appear as married Mrs. Sponge living with bachelor Romford. They finally decide that Lucy can pass as Facey's half-sister, Mrs. Somerville, widow of an Indian officer. She becomes irresistibly intriguing to the neighborhood when the rumor circulates that she has £10,000 a year which she forfeits if she remarries. This imaginary income is sure to win her ardent admirers, while the stipulation attached keeps her free from embarrassing marriage proposals which might necessitate the ruinous confession that she is already married or might lead to an investigation of her background.

Surtees did not leave all flirtation and courtship behind in *Ask Mamma* and *Plain or Ringlets*, however, for Facey appears to the parents of marriageable daughters as an extremely fine prospect for a son-in-law. Before long he is the object of competition between two lovely young women, Anna Maria Hazey and Cassandra Cleopatra Watkins. Watching these two minxes vie for the attentions of the great bear Romford, who is constantly vacillating between them, is one of the novel's delights. There is one major difference, however, between the way courtship is presented here and the way it was handled in *Ask Mamma* and *Plain or Ringlets*; in this novel such activity is restricted to the drawing room and dining room, extending to hunt dinners and hunt breakfasts, perhaps, but never onto the hunting field itself. Surtees felt that he had made his point about this particular perverted use of hunting, and the people in *Mr. Romford*, for the most part, hunt only for love of the sport, and not to capture a mate, to advance social position, or to sell a horse.

Facey and Lucy take Doubleimupshire absolutely by storm. Granted Facey seems to the local residents a bit eccentric ("Some said he was a bear, others that he was a beau. There was a great difference of opinion"—187) but then they all conform to the popular belief that truly wealthy men usually have certain peculiarities. Besides, he is an excellent master of hounds who hunts the country at his own expense and never fails to show them a good day's sport. Lucy wins unanimous approval, her acting ability and common sense convincing everyone she meets that she has lived her whole life in luxury and ease. She, especially, makes liberal use of the Romford seal to procure them both the finest clothes, food, and hunting accessories. As Mr. Noakes reminds the reader, "Once again Surtees plays his familiar trick of demonstrating that nothing helps a rogue to impose on his victims more than the cupidity or the

snobbery of the victims themselves."[7] Facey and Lucy have learned
the lessons of Minshull Vernon; Facey overcomes the temptation to
make precarious horse sales, and Lucy stays out of the hunting field
except for occasional forays with Facey alone. Their popularity
reaches majestic heights when they host a sumptuous dinner and
grand ball, charged to the "Turbot upon its tail," of course, for
more than seventy of the local gentry.

Everything seems to be going their way, and the longer they
succeed in their charade the more convinced they and the reader
become that the good life can last forever. After a period of time
they begin to get careless, inviting to visit them Lucy's actress
friend Betsy Shannon, whom they masquerade as Miss Hamilton
Howard on the premise that "what would have been downright
vulgarity in a Shannon, became the easy manners of high life with a
Howard" (318). Even Mr. Goodhearted Green, the London horse-
dealer, pays a visit, and he becomes Sir Roger Ferguson.

Certainly, amongst them our friends at Beldon Hall combined as much
duplicity as could well be contained in a party of four. First there was Mr.
Romford, acting the turbot-on-its-tail, deceiving poor Lord Lovetin, Lord
Lonnergan, and all; then there was Mrs. Sponge, calling herself Mrs.
Somerville, and Betsy Shannon, arrogating the distinguished name of
Hamilton Howard; and now the old Clerkenwell " 'oss dealer," Mr.
Goodhearted Green, passing himself off for a baronet. All or any were liable
to be detected at any moment—Mr. Romford by Lord Lovetin's making his
long-meditated journey to England, Mrs. Somerville by the frequenters of
theatres and cigar shops, Miss Shannon by half the counter-skippers in London, and Sir Roger Ferguson by any stray tourist or stableman with whom
he had ever done business (370).

By this time *Mr. Romford* has assumed all the false identities,
humor, and suspense of a drawing-room comedy.

And in the best drawing-room comedy tradition, everything is
unraveled at the end. The revelations start when Lucy is prevailed
upon to sell that mischievous horse Leotard again, this time out of
the country, for the horse passes through the hands of many go-
betweens before it reaches its new owner, the Countess of
Caperington. From Lucy's viewpoint nothing could be more safe.
What she cannot possibly know is that the Countess of Caperington
is none other than the former actress Miss Spangles, who had
become the wife of Sir Harry Scattercash of Nonsuch House. It was

as a guest of her old friend Lady Scattercash that Lucy had met Soapey Sponge. After Lucy married Sponge and left for London, "worn out with debauchery and premature decay, Sir Harry Scattercash presently departed this life at the early age of thirty two" (373 - 374), and his grieving widow eventually became the bride of the Earl of Caperington. When the irascible Leotard throws her in the mud, she not only returns the horse, but also sets out herself for Doubleimupshire to avenge her injured pride. The inevitable confrontation takes place just as Lucy is riding out on Leotard to wish her "brother's" followers a good day of hunting.

Lucy wondered who the strangers were—then she thought she had seen that face before—very likely Lady Scattercash's—couldn't be Lady Scattercash—yes it was Lady Scattercash. "How do you do, Lady Scattercash?" said she, riding up to the carriage-door and tendering her hand as she spoke. But the Countess, who had had the advantage of a quiet carriage-seat for the survey, had realized Lucy before Lucy did her, and her displeasure at seeing the horse going so quietly was not at all diminished by the familiarity of *that person* calling her Lady Scattercash, when she was in fact the Countess of Caperington. So she neglected the proffered hand and preserved a stolid scornful stare. "I think you don't know me," said Lucy, timidly, withdrawing her hand as she spoke. "Yes, I do," replied the Countess, haughtily, "You are Mrs. Sponge—Lucy Glitters that was—most pernicious woman!"

Poor Lucy is undone. "If the Countess had stabbed her to the heart she could not have inflicted a more deadly wound, for there were horsemen all around, every one of whom, Lucy felt sure, would hear what was said. The words perfectly rang in her ears—'You are Mrs. Sponge—Lucy Glitters that was—most pernicious woman!' She was indeed Mrs. Sponge—Lucy Glitters that was; but she felt that it was not for an old comrade like Lady Scattercash to upbraid her. She would not have done so by the Countess. And, turning her horse short round, poor Lucy burst into a flood of tears" (392). When Lucy cries, says a reviewer in the *Times Literary Supplement,* "we have the nearest approach to tragedy that Surtees admits."[8]

Facey decides to brazen it out, and may have succeeded had it not been for the second catastrophe, the long-dreaded arrival of Lord Lovetin, whose curiosity concerning his tenant has been aroused by his nonpayment of the quarterly rent. Now it is Facey's turn to be discovered.

However much boys may change as they grow into men, there will generally be some distinguishing feature by which they can be recognised; but under no possible process could the little dark-beady black-eyed Romford of
his Lordship's early days have grown up into the great Herculean monster
that now arose from his lair before him. His Lordship started, for he
thought to give his old schoolfellow an agreeable surprise; and Romford
started, for he was not accustomed to intruders, and didn't want to be
troubled. They then stood staring at one another like Spanish pointers, each
wondering who the other was. Lord Lovetin at length broke silence.
    "Beg pardon," said he, "but I thought it was Mr. Romford." "Romford it
is." said Facey, yawning, and stretching out his great arms as if to show the
intruder what he had to contend with . . . "But not the Romford I was at
school with," observed his Lordship, eyeing him intently. "Don't know
who you are, to begin with," replied Facey; "but moy name's Romford,"
observed he; "*that oi'll swear to.*" "I'm Lord Lovetin," replied his
Lordship, mildly. If his Lordship had put a pistol to our Master's head he
could not have given him a greater shock; and forthwith all his acts of omis-
sion and commission rushed to his mind with terrible velocity: the trifle of
rent, the conversion of the coach-horses, the spurious sister, the turbot-on-
its-tail seal (397 - 398).

The game is up, but by no means can Facey and Lucy be considered the losers. First Facey demands, and receives, from the
weak Lovetin not only the dismissal of all back rent, but also, since
Lovetin wants to break his lease, a handsome bonus for going away.
Before they leave they see Miss Hamilton Howard, really Miss Betsy Shannon, married clandestinely to the wealthy Mr. Lovetin
Lonnergan under the supposedly assumed name of Elizabeth Shannon, and Facey himself brings to a close his dual courtship with his
hasty marriage to the heiress Miss Cassandra Cleopatra Watkins.
Meanwhile the news has reached Lucy that her errant husband,
Soapey Sponge, has turned up in Australia, much better off for having found a few gold nuggets. Lucy decides to "share the success of
her Sponge" (404) and sets off for the Antipodes, where she and
Sponge are joined by Facey and his bride, who have come to
superintend the Watkins family's investment on that continent.
"The last account heard of Soapey and him was that they were going to set up a bank in Collins Street East, under the firm of 'Romford and Sponge.' Good luck attend their exertions, say we! We expect to hear of their setting up a pack of hounds together next"
(405).
    Although *Handley Cross* and *Mr. Sponge's Sporting Tour* have
always been Surtees's most popular books, *Mr. Romford's Hounds*

is in many ways a better novel, most obviously because it has two features which all Surtees's earlier novels lack: a new, more human hero, and Surtees's *only* fully drawn, realistic female character.

Although Facey Romford is another of Surtees's great hero-villains, he is neither so arrogant as John Jorrocks nor so self-assertive as Soapey Sponge. While it is true that he takes advantage of the coincidence concerning his name and trades upon the borrowed Romford crest, he never actually *tells* anyone he is the other Romford—he simply lets other people draw the wrong conclusions and does nothing to correct them. As Surtees insists, when a wealthy bachelor, a man who is a fine huntsman and giver of grand parties, is in question, people are every bit as willing to be deceived as Facey is to deceive them. He never pushes himself into people's homes, as Sponge does, or takes advantage of their friendship, as Jorrocks tends to do. Even the questionable horse deals in which he participates are not initiated by him; he merely accepts the offers other people make. If those offers happen to be ridiculous, they are not his responsibility. He simply wants to be able to live comfortably, lamb chops and batter pudding constituting his favorite meal. He has no social pretension; he rents Beldon Hall unseen simply because it is available, and his first sight of so much grandeur genuinely dismays him. " 'A house is a consuming animal,' he always said. He liked the simplicity of the Dog and Partridge Inn, and the easy independence of the 'West-end Swell.' However, he was in for it, and must brazen it out. He wasn't easily cowed" (107).

Unlike Soapey Sponge, who hunts primarily to show off a horse he wants to sell, Facey lives to hunt, and the social and economic responsibilities incumbent on a master of hounds are simply to be endured. He would much rather stay at home in the evening with his pipe and a bottle of Lovetin's gin than face a dinner party; in fact, if it were not for Lucy's nagging he probably would never have gone out at all. For example, when he and Lucy receive their first invitation he tries every excuse he can invent to get out of it. "He didn't feel comfortable out, he said. . . . Then Facey hadn't a dress coat. . . . The women bothered him. He didn't know what to say to them. He didn't know how to get them in to dinner. He didn't know how to get them out again" (186). Lucy has an answer for every objection, "and so poor Facey was at length obliged to submit . . . thinking that life would be very pleasant if it were not for its enjoyments" (190).

Another beautiful example of Facey's overwhelming desire to be left alone is the scene in which Lucy shows the Watkins women through the house on their first visit and poor Facey, trying to keep out of sight, is driven from room to room ahead of them and finally into the scullery. In desperation he clambers up the coal-cellar grate and, "mistaking the side of the cellers, crawled out right in front of the Watkins' horses' heads, to the astonishment of Mr. Spanker and the magnificent footman. . . . Not being, however, easily disconcerted, friend Facey just asked them, in a careless indifferent sort of way, if they had seen a rat come up, and, being answered in the negative, he turned in again at a side door as if nothing particular had happened" (142). W. C. Rivers characterizes him, rather affectionately, one feels, as "Facey Romford, the sportsman who seems in essentials so near the cave man. . . . With his hunting craft and his weapons, his laziness about everything else save his flute, his what we consider knavery, even his red hair (primitive man was rufous), Facey is the savage to the life, a reversion, an atavism, 'rude, crude, naked force.' "[9]

Facey has little in common with Jorrocks and even less with that pushier version of Jorrocks, Soapey Sponge. He would rather die than deliver a "sporting lector," rather leave the country than impose himself on a Duke of Donkeyton. The very idea of running for public office would give him nightmares. He values his privacy much too dearly to surrender it to the Puffingtons, Crowdeys, and Scattercashs of the world, even in exchange for free room and board. On the other hand he is certainly a far cry from the innocuous Tom Scott, the dumb Billy Pringle, or the dandy Jack Bunting. He is a new kind of hero for Surtees, an individual, a believable human being, more low-key than Jorrocks and more likable than Sponge, further from a stereotype than any he had yet produced.

Perhaps Surtees's distinction between his natural men and his artificial ones is best made in this novel, for although *Mr. Romford* really has fewer minor characters to demonstrate the difference satirically than many of Surtees's other novels, the author provides instead a spokesman in Independent Jimmy, the bus and "chay" driver who articulates, after a fashion, many of Surtees's own values. Jimmy is a kind of working-class Romford, a "big, burly, strongly-built blunt Northumbrian" who "never said Sir, or Ma'am, or Miss, or used any of the circumlocutory forms of address, but just blurted out, 'Noo then!' 'Get oop!' 'Get doon!' 'Get in!' 'Get oot!' and shoved his passengers about like so many sheep" (102). He is a particularly astute judge of human character and in Romford he recognizes at first glance another "independent" like himself, "not a man of much blandishment, ar should say" (108). As he drives Romford and Lucy to Beldon Hall upon their arrival in Doubleimupshire he describes for their benefit the local citizens, revealing in the process their assets and defects, assigning them their true characters, which they are destined to reveal in the course of the novel. Mr. Watkins, for example, is another of Surtees's pseudogentry, *nouveau riche*, a man who, like Muleygrubs and Mainchance before him, acquired his money in business and then set out, like Nosey Brown, to "ape a country gentleman." "Leuk, noo," points out Independent Jimmy as they pass the Watkins estate, "at them there lodges with the red and gould lion crests and grand fancy gates, just as if they belanged to a duke." Jimmy classifies Watkins and his family as "the biggest feuls in arl the country." Their daughter, Romford's future wife, is, according to Jimmy, "the impittantest, sarciest gal i' the world." "Sink, I'd skelp her ivry other day gin she were mine," he grumbles. Mr. Hazey is another kind of "imposition," a man who has money but refuses to spend it, "quite a wonderful sort of man for meanness," says Jimmy, who then asks the question Surtees hopes his readers will ask themselves before they finish the novel: "But what signifies his riches; does things that a beggar would be sham'd on." Next to these Jimmy contrasts a *real* gentleman. "Noo this be a gentleman comin'," he warns Romford, pointing out "a sporting-like man in leather leggings and a shooting-jacket." Such men do not need external show or feigned snobbery, "powdered footmen nor piebald gates," to prove their worth. In three sentences Independent Jimmy makes a final indictment against Surtees's, and the world's, phonies: "Sink, but ar often wonders who those sort o' fondies think they impose upon. It can't be the likes of me . . . for we know all about them; it can't be the gentlefolks, for they'll ha nout to say to them. It mun just be their arn silly sels" (103 - 106).

This characterization certainly does not fit Romford, for even his own great affair, the catered dinner and grand ball, comes as a complete surprise to Facey. Lucy and friend Betsy persuade him to agree to an "at home," which they define as "a little music here some evening" with "a little tea and coffee" and "p'r'aps a sandwich and a glass of sherry before they go away." Facey agrees on certain conditions: he will be able to play his flute for the company, men will be invited along with the ladies so that it will not turn into a "hen party," the guests will not get into his bedroom, he will not be required to make a speech, and "rabbit-poie and cheese" will be substituted for the more expensive sandwiches (320 - 321). When he realizes in the middle of it that the whole affair has grown considerably beyond his expectations, his sole concern is for the expense. "Mr. Romford started convulsively when he got to the dining-room door . . . for, however bold the Beldon Hall ladies were, he did not think they dared have ventured on such a step as this" (340). He wanders around stunned, muttering to himself, " 'Where the devil do the chickens come from? where the deuce do the hams come from? where the dickens do the turkeys come from?' . . . And Facey felt just as if he was going to get a stomach-ache" (340). He drinks enough champagne to cure his stomach, however, and the lovely Misses Watkins and Hazey divert his attention from his pocketbook to themselves. For the rest of the evening he just shakes his head in wonder and thinks over and over that "the ways of women are wonderful" (337).

Whether Surtees himself agreed that "the ways of women are wonderful" is certainly open to serious question, for his treatment of women as characters in his novels has earned him severe criticism from every person who has written about his work. Not until Lucy Glitters in *Mr. Romford* did Surtees create a woman character in any depth; even more serious, not until Lucy Glitters did Surtees present or even mention women for any purpose other than to demean them or to laugh at them.

There has been among critics considerable discussion concerning the possible reasons for his apparently bitter attitude toward women. "Surely there has never been a novelist of the same importance who knew or cared so little about women,"[10] states Mr. Cooper. Surtees, like Jorrocks, must have considered women to be "werry weary warmints."[11] Cooper speculates whether the cause may be found in the male-dominated Hamsterley environment of Surtees's early childhood or whether Surtees may simply have been influenced, as all artists and especially satirists are to some extent, by the prevailing sense of humor of his times.

It is poor, unworthy humour and he works it to death, but his attitude towards women is always one of the less pleasing things about him. It is some excuse for him that this type of humor was current coin of his contemporaries. Nothing apparently delighted the Victorians more than the perfectly natural and sometimes pathetic phenomenon of an unmarried girl wanting a man. If in addition the girl were ageing or unattractive the jest was even more exquisite. . . . Surtees, though he differed from the Victorians in so many ways, adopted this convention. Probably he was so little interested in women and knew so little about them that it saved him trouble to use the popular form of humour, but it is hardly to his credit either as a man or as a writer.[12]

At any rate, Surtees certainly fell victim over and over again to the most degrading of female stereotypes, for all of his women except Lucy Glitters Sponge are two-dimensional and easily categorized. Among his major female characters there are just two types—the marriage-minded "mamma" trying to sell her offspring to the highest bidder (Mrs. Flather, Mrs. Trotter, Mrs. McDermott, and Mrs. Jorrocks with her neice Belinda, as well as that most famous mother of all, Mrs. Pringle) and the marriageable daughter who is perfectly willing to be sold for the best settlement (Emma Flather, Angelina Blunt, Rosa McDermott, Cassandra Cleopatra Watkins, Anna Maria Hazey). Although these are obviously stereotypes, at least Surtees allows them to play conspicuous roles in his works; all his other women are not only stereotypes but also so constricted in their presentation that they never rise above a caricature. Women servants are dirty, lazy thieves. Young girls, while sometimes physically attractive, are always superficial and fickle with minds obsessed with marriage and clothes; in fact, they are never allowed to think one thought not directly connected with those two subjects. Once the girls are married they turn into shrews just like their mothers.

Women are, in other words, a nuisance. They perpetuate conversation at the dinner table when the men want to stuff themselves in peace and quiet; they wear crinolines and hoop-skirts that fill up the inside of a carriage, leaving no room for the men; they insist on having a new dress once in a while. Only one male character, the Marquis of Bray in *Hillingdon Hall*, does not breathe a sigh of relief when the women retire to the drawing room after dinner—in fact, "not being a great man for his liquor"[13] he actually sneaks away from the table and joins them! But then Surtees makes clear that there is some question about the Marquis's masculinity anyway, referring to him as "the butterfly Marquis"[14] and asserting that "Nature meant the Marquis for a girl, and a very pretty one he would have made."[15] After all, no one "of the breeches, at least *legitimately* of the breeches,"[16] would have acted in such a manner.

It would not be valid to argue that Surtees was writing satire and was, therefore, just as hard on the men. He was not. While it is true that many of his male characters are obviously satirical caricature or "humour" characters, even they show more variety and more believable human qualities than do any of his women. In fact, all characters with any imagination, any integrity, any sensitivity, even any intelligence, are men. "All Surtees' girls are nasty little monkeys, without heart or passion, however pretty they may be . . . all his women aspire meanly after mean things."[17] It would not be surprising if all Surtees's female readers, after such a display as this, would agree with Lucy who "often said that the only thing that reconciled her to being a woman was, that she could not by any possibility have to marry one" (257).

Then suddenly, with this kind of record in the presentation of women, Surtees, in his last novel, came up with a Lucy Glitters Sponge Somerville Sponge. What a delight and what a relief! She is everything the most ardent feminist of today could ask for. She is strong, independent, and hard-working. When the cigar store is in jeopardy and her husband completely irresponsible she goes on trying to make it work. When Sponge runs off she quietly salvages what she can for herself and retires to suffer in private whatever feelings of anger or sense of loss may assail her. She is beautiful and proud of her beauty in the best sense—she dresses well because it makes her feel good about herself; she accepts admiration gracefully but never demands it. She is genuinely fond of Facey and manages, because of her attachment and endless patience, to civilize him. She supports her mother and entertains her friends in style. She is aware of all the stereotypes usually associated with her sex and uses them, sometimes necessarily and sometimes for fun—she can be the coquette or the little girl or the nagging wife or the dumb blonde when assuming those roles will get her what she wants or protect herself or Facey from exposure. Underneath that pretty, feminine exterior she is as intelligent, independent, and tough-minded as any person can be. "As a leading lady," states Cooper, "she is superb."[18] Watson goes further and ranks Lucy with the best of Surtees's unconventional characters, with John Jorrocks, with Soapey Sponge, with Facey Romford himself.

Because of her artistic temperament—now so much better understood—and her indifference to the conventions Lucy Glitters has joined the great company of Surtees' characters, of whom it has been said by prudish persons that they are all impossible "to admire." Let it be allowed that the faculty of admiration is a pleasant emotion, but hero-worship is not everything. To regard a character in fiction with affection or amusement, instead of reverence, may not be so dignified, but it is less strenuous. There are quite a number of people who may not admire Lucy Glitters, but surely the time has arrived to admit that she will stand fire as an attractive, lifelike, and lovable character? Surtees calls Lucy "*tolerably* virtuous." Was she the worse for that? There are plenty of intolerably virtuous to satisfy the pure in heart.[19]

Those "pure in heart" had already been administered a jolt by Surtees in a particularly explicit bit of dialogue in *Mr. Sponge;* if they took exception to that and to the character of Lucy, it is probably fortunate that they had no way of knowing how narrowly they were spared the inconvenience of moral outrage. The dialogue in *Mr. Sponge* occurs between the actress Miss Howard, a guest at Nonsuch House, and a neighborhood youngster who refuses an invitation to enter the house because "Mar said we hadn't . . . she said the house was full of trumpets."[20] That suggestion of illicit sexual activity was nothing compared to what Surtees was contemplating for his readers of *Mr. Romford!* Mr. Johnston-Jones, after studying recently discovered proof pages for eight chapters of that novel, reports "that Surtees was originally far more explicit in his acknowledgement of the sexual relationship between Romford and Mrs. Sponge. In the printed version this relationship is only implied, whereas the proof indicates it quite clearly. . . . It is pretty clear . . . that in the original version of the story Lucy Sponge is Romford's mistress at the time of his becoming Master of the Heavyside Hounds. It would indeed seem reasonable to assume that she went to live with him as soon as Sponge left her."[21] Again Surtees saved his novel (or so his contemporaries would have believed) and, in this case, his reputation as a result of his careful literary judgment.

All things considered, *Mr. Romford's Hounds,* Surtees's last book, is also his best. It has more structure, more plot, than any of the others. It has genuine suspense created by the assumption of false identities which the reader knows will have to be uncovered. Its hunting scenes have all the color and excitement of those of *Handley Cross* and the "wheeling and dealing," if less prominent, is every bit as clever as in *Mr. Sponge.* Those intimate details of Victorian life, from the discomforts of the "melon-frame" buggy to the dingy bedrooms, from the elaborate dinners to the smoky candles, from the glorious dress to the filthy servants, were never better represented. In contrast to the last three novels particularly, the humor has lost its bitterness and the satire its maliciousness. Facey Romford and Lucy Glitters outshine all Surtees's earlier characters. Perhaps his turning from fiction to autobiography was evidence of his own satisfaction, his recognition that he had reached a plateau, that all those characters and methods that he had been experimenting with over the last thirty-three years, ever since the first Jorrocks story appeared in the *New Sporting Magazine*, had finally come together and worked just right.

CHAPTER 6

Surtees in Retrospect

Y ES, Mrs. Roosevelt and I are both as fond as you are of the immortal "Soapey Sponge," but I shall be very grateful if you will send me that copy, because the only copy we have in the house is one Mrs. Roosevelt inherited from her father. It is a rather cheap American edition, though with the Leech pictures, and we have read it until it has practically tumbled to pieces.

President Theodore Roosevelt, 1906[1]

I *Surtees: His Readers and Critics*

Robert Smith Surtees has never enjoyed widespread critical acclaim, or, for that matter, even widespread critical attention. He has, however, consistently held through the last century the esteem of a group of readers surprisingly large considering the narrow scope of the subject matter of his novels. Many of those readers have, of course, been fox-hunters, but many others have never seen a hunt nor ridden a horse. In some cases, like Mrs. Roosevelt's, people have grown up reading Surtees's works and inherited them along with the family silver. In other instances readers found their way to Surtees's works by way of Dickens, Thackeray, or Sassoon. Some people have had Surtees fairly foisted upon them by friends who are Surtees enthusiasts, as did Arnold Bennett, who asked Siegfried Sassoon one day whether Surtees could "really be perused." "Whereupon," reports Sassoon, "I went straight to a bookstore and ordered *Sponge* and *Romford* to be sent to him. A few days later I received a postcard. 'Many thanks for putting me right on Surtees. *Romford* is the real thing.' "[2]

During his own lifetime, most of Surtees's reward for his literary labors came not from recognized literary critics but rather from the successful sale of his books, especially after *Mr. Sponge's Sporting Tour* caught the public's attention and *Handley Cross*, reissued

with Leech prints, became popular. He might well have been amused by some aspects of that popularity, such as the publication of the
"Ask Mamma Polka" and the annual insertion by the hunting
editor of the *Field* of a note to his contributors warning them to use
no "threadbare Jorrocks witticisms."³ Even more gratifying,
however, must have been the praise of his personal friends, many of
whom were themselves writers. For example, shortly after making
Surtees's acquaintance William Thackeray wrote to confess: "Mr.
Jorrocks has long been a dear and intimate friend of mine. I stole
from him years ago, having to describe a hunting scene with which
I was quite unfamiliar, and I lived in Great Coram Street once
too."⁴ His letter upon receipt of several chapters of *Mr. Sponge* is
indicative of his enthusiasm. "This is not to thank you for the
grouse," he wrote, "but for the last two numbers of 'Soapey
Sponge': they are capital, and the Flat Hats delightful; those
fellows in spectacles divine; and Scamperdale's character perfectly
odious and admirable."⁵

Another famous writer whose entire literary career may be said to
stem from the popularity of Surtees is Charles Dickens, for his early
novel *The Posthumous Papers of the Pickwick Club* was composed
of sketches intended to accompany Robert Seymour's drawings ("a
running accompaniment—like an ornamental border round the
drawings"⁶) of a middle-aged, overweight Cockney sportsman, a
character type introduced to the literary world five years earlier in
the form of John Jorrocks. Like Jorrocks in *Jaunts*, Pickwick sets out
to investigate scenes of popular entertainment. Like Jorrocks, he has
a series of adventures and misadventures, including a shooting accident. And like Jorrocks, he runs afoul the law and has his day in
court, where he is defended by a lawyer modeled after the identical
person who served as Surtees's original. Whether the young
Dickens had ever actually read Surtees's *Jaunts* is impossible to
determine, but it was no doubt the popularity of the Jorrocks
sketches in the *New Sporting* that encouraged Chapman and Hall
to publish the Seymour drawings; thus, at least indirectly, Surtees
was influential in establishing the career of one of England's finest
and most successful writers.

It is interesting to note the influence Surtees was to have on
writers who were not his contemporaries. Siegfried Sassoon, for instance, was one of those who knew the works of Surtees from
childhood.

We adopted and matured a specialized jargon drawn almost exclusively from the characters in the novels of Surtees; since we knew these almost by heart, they provided us with something like a dialect of our own, and in our carefree moments we exchanged remarks in the mid-Victorian language of such character-parts as Mr. Romford, Major Yammerton, and Sir Moses Mainchance, while Mr. Jorrocks was an all-pervading influence. In our Surtees obsession we went so far that we almost identified ourselves with certain characters on appropriate occasions. One favourite role which Stephen facetiously imposed on me was that of a young gentleman named Billy Pringle. . . .[7]

"For me, as for previous generations of Surteesians," he wrote later in his introduction to *Hunting Scenes from Surtees*, "the only thing wrong about his books is that I have read them too often and know them too well."[8]

Another, perhaps more surprising, Surtees admirer was Nobel Prize - winner Rudyard Kipling, who not only made frequent references to and quoted liberally from Surtees, but also in one of his stories, "My Son's Wife," wrote about the novels directly. His main character, Midmore, stumbles across one of the Jorrocks trilogy.

He began at random and read a little, moved into the drawing-room with the volume, and settled down by the fire still reading. It was a foul world into which he peeped for the first time—a heavy-eating, hard-drinking hell of horse-copers, swindlers, matchmaking mothers, economically dependent virgins selling themselves blushingly for cash and lands: Jews, tradesmen, and an ill-considered spawn of Dickens-and-horsedung characters . . . but he read on, fascinated. . . . Outrageous as thought and conception were, the stuff seemed to have the rudiments of observation. He dug out other volumes by the same author . . . and went to bed with a book called *Handley Cross* under his arm, and a lonelier Columbus into a stranger world the wet-ringed moon never looked upon.[9]

After the city-bred Midmore becomes better acquainted with his new country neighbors, he "would go home and identify them, one by one, out of the natural-history books by Mr. Surtees. . . ."[10]

The critics, however, did not take to Surtees with as much enthusiasm as did his readers—in fact, most of them seem almost to have been dragged reluctantly along in the wake of what came to be known as the "Surtees habit." Sir Arthur Quiller-Couch, for example, found him "not a great writer, but to me, to this day, a very amusing one."[11] George Saintsbury in *The English Novel* described

him as "nearly always readable and sometimes very amusing." [12]
Some critics have even gone so far as to account for his popularity
solely on the basis of the Leech drawings. Their thinking has at least
two fallacies: first, other books illustrated by Leech, John Mill's
Flyers of the Hunt, for example, have fallen into oblivion despite
their illustration; and second, Surtees's novels continue to sell in all
editions including those illustrated by modern artists and those with
no illustrations at all. In 1913 Moira O'Neill, writing in *Blackwood's
Magazine,* took all such critics to task. "If the literary world has
been foolish enough to overlook Surtees, the ordinary world, which
after all has more people in it, has shown better sense. What books
are taken oftener from the shelves in the smoking-room than those
thick volumes in the cheerful red, 'Handley Cross' and 'Mr.
Sponge's Sporting Tour'?" [13]

There were two happy exceptions during Surtees's lifetime to this
critical trend, however. One occurred in *Fraser's Magazine* in an article entitled "Sporting Literature" in October 1838. "With the
New Sporting Magazine may be ascribed the birth of what may be
called a school of sporting fiction. . . . each sketch is done in a
style to interest the general reader, as well as the lover of the particular amusement. The scene at Newmarket, where the honest
grocer joins a party of blacklegs at the White Hart, conveys a better
idea of the doings of that noted spot than any we have ever read."
The article goes on to compare Jorrocks with Pickwick, concluding
that "Pickwick is an excellent character, with the assistance of Sam
Weller; but, viewed singly, Jorrocks, in our opinion, is the better of
the two." [14] The other predominatly positive review was that same
Quarterly Review article which directed Surtees to "curb his
propensity to caricature." Mr. Lockhart wrote, "An amusing book
might be written on the 'genuine sportsmen' of this our great city;
and we heartily wish Mr. Surtees of Hamsterley Hall,
Northumberland, for whom we are indebted for the volumes named
at the head of this paper, would undertake the job . . . the easy
style in which he arranges and draws out his characters convinces us
that he might, if he pleased, take a high place among our modern
novelists. He has a world of knowledge of life and manners beyond
what most of those now in vogue can pretend to; and a gentleman-
like tone and spirit, perhaps even rarer among them." [15]

There are two aspects of Surtees's writing which probably account for much of the general lack of critical attention: first, as a
"sporting author" he was undoubtedly considered "light-weight"

by those who thought of themselves as serious scholars of literature; and as a satirist who insisted on remaining loyal to his own ideals rather than counterfeiting those of his age, he frequently seemed to fly in the face of the conservative moral tone espoused by his contemporaries. Ernest A. Baker, writing in *The History of the English Novel*, came to the same conclusion:

Surtees was not welcomed by the lover of light literature in his own time or by his fellow-sportsmen; *Handley Cross* and *Hillingdon Hall* were a long time coming into their own. Perhaps it was partly that he knew too much; his legal information was astounding, and he did not spare his readers in this or any other branch of his technical knowledge. *Handley Cross* is a veritable text-book of fox-hunting, and it would be risky to suggest that any single one of the rest is less thorough. He did not like the fashionable crowd, and the fashionable crowd did not like him. He was a bluff old philistine who must have seemed a downright cynic to the mid-Victorians. The sporting crowd soon found themselves in a position to show their preference for his younger rival, Whyte-Melville, who was more of their caste and temper than the man who had stamped some decisive impression of himself on that rich blend of horse-sense, personal competence, and contemptuous self-respect, Mr. Jorrocks.[16]

Mr. Frederick Watson adds still another consideration: "When an anonymous writer on fox-hunting works in the same period as the Brontes, George Eliot, Mrs. Gaskell, Dickens, Thackeray, Lytton, Ainsworth, Tennyson, and the rest of them he must bide his time. Between the years 1858 and 1861, when *Ask Mamma* and *Plain or Ringlets* were published, there came out, like moral explosives, *Adam Bede*, *The Mill on the Floss*, *Framley Parsonage*, *Great Expectations*, and *The Cloister and the Hearth*. Heavy artillery against a hunting satirist in an earnest age!"[17]

"Heavy artillery" or not, critical acclaim or none, the novels of Robert Smith Surtees were, and are, read. "Those who do not read the novels of Surtees never think of him at all," states Moira O'Neill. "Those who do read the novels of Surtees never forget him."[18]

II   *Surtees and the Modern Reader*

More than a century after his death, Robert Smith Surtees is still far from what would be considered a "popular" writer. Now, however, the majority of books on Victorian literature make some mention of him and at least two doctoral dissertations, those of Ms. Hallgarth and Mr. Johnston-Jones (the latter published), have been written about him in the last ten years. That might not be overwhelming critical progress, but progress it is, especially when one considers the vast numbers of novelists who have disappeared entirely from view during those intervening decades. What is more, Surtees's novels are still enjoyed by a readership relatively small but truly admiring—in that regard it is interesting to note that at this date it is harder to find a person who has read just one novel of Surtees than it is to find one who has read just one novel of Dickens.

There is much in the works of Surtees to appeal to the modern reader. Chief among his attributes is his gift of characterization; once one encounters the characters of Surtees they are with him forever. John Jorrocks is undoubtedly the best known because *Handley Cross* remains Surtees's most popular book, but Soapey Sponge and Facey Romford and Lucy Glitters are equally unforgettable. One would expect to remember main characters created by any good novelist, however; what is almost unique about Surtees is that so many of his minor characters carry the same impact. The wheezing Jogglebury Crowdey with his house full of "gibbey sticks"; poor nearsighted Jack Spraggon, "turning his eyes inside-out" in his attempts to see clearly; the decadents of Nonsuch House with their perpetual delirium tremens; Jean Rougier, who loses his phony French accent when he gets excited; that fat "monster" Colonel Blunt; Cuddy Flintoff, whose "sporting was all in the past tense"; even the lovely "Dirtiest of the Dirty" stay forever in the reader's memory, lurking somewhere in the background of consciousness to be brought forth and enjoyed at will.

Another aspect of Surtees's writing which is both delightful and instructive is the marvelous picture he gives of Victorian life, not as it was colored by the emotion or romanticized by the action of so many popular Victorian novels, but as it was lived from day to day. From dingy bedrooms of country houses to filthy stables of country inns, from fashionable promenades in vacation resorts to bloody scenes in dog-fighting pits, from hunting field to dinner tables Surtees shows it all just as it really was. Considering all his works together, one can say without reservation that no other single writer has presented Victorian life in more vivid or realistic detail. And especially in his descriptions of food and clothes, the enormous breakfasts and ten-course dinners, the endless toasting and continual drinking, the foppery of the "swell" and dirty moleskins of the currant-jelly men, he is absolutely unsurpassed.

One may also point to Surtees's dialogue as one of his great accomplishments. "The great Victorians, with all their merits, were as a rule indifferent writers of dialogue," states Cooper. "They seemed to ignore the fundamental fact that men and women in ordinary conversation do not talk coherent prose. Their characters could hardly say good-morning to each other without making a speech about it. . . . But Surtees really did know how people talked. From the earliest discussion at the meet in the *Jaunts and Jollities* to the last talk in *Mr. Romford* the books are crammed with dialogue of the very best sort—crisp, accurate, colloquial, amusing and above all natural.''[19] He goes on to explain the difference between dialogue that strains to be humorous and the dialogue of humorous characters.

There is no exaggeration in Surtees' dialogue, which is often at its best in the quieter passages. He is not obliged to force the comic relief since there is nothing in the books that needs relief, and so it follows that his characters are talking in their normal accents and at their normal level. There is no virtuosity in the dialogue itself. With the exception of Mr. Jorrocks, who was a humorist in word as well as in deed, there is hardly a character whose speech is worth quoting as purely humorous dialogue. It is too natural, too life-like. It is always the speech of characters humorous in themselves, who have no need of verbal fireworks.[20]

Finally, one must consider Surtees's style. It is true that in terms of the smaller niceties he was no great stylist: his transitions in time and place are almost always mechanical and frequently awkward; his tenses jump around disconcertingly; he overuses clichés and onomatopoeia; he grows particularly careless of grammar and diction in those parts of his books which interest him least; he does not, in short, always dot his literary "i's" or cross his literary "t's." But he has something else which more than makes up for these oversights; one of the highest tributes to the style of Surtees and other sporting writers came from one who had no personal affinity for sports but who was, unquestionably, one of the greatest stylists in the history of English literature—Virginia Woolf. "Indeed," she writes in the *Common Reader*, "the English Sporting writers, Beckford, St. John, Surtees, Nimrod make no mean reading. In their slapdash, gentlemanly way they have ridden their pens as boldly as they have ridden their horses. They have had their effect upon the language. This riding and tumbling, this being blown upon and

rained upon and splashed from head to heels with mud, have worked themselves into the very texture of English prose."21 Leonard
Cooper singles out Surtees for praise, seeing him as instrumental in
shaping the direction of the English novel. "Whatever the late Victorians contributed to the English novel, their effect on its style was
not wholly to its advantage. Too often the writing became heavy,
the tone didactic, the sentimentality cloying. Far too often, under
the disguise of the novel, lurked the tract and the sermon. The
broad jollity of *Handley Cross*, the astringency of Soapey Sponge
and Facey Romford were needed to preserve the balance, to enable
a later generation to be profound without being portentous and to
present psychology without losing all sight of humor. And humor is
the greatest legacy which Surtees left to the English novel."22

In considering the place of Robert Smith Surtees in the history of
English literature, it is gratifying to contrast the high opinion which
modern critics hold for the works of Surtees with those reluctant
words of praise awarded him by critics in his own day. "What is it in
Surtees' more popular novels which still attracts the ordinary
reader?" asked Frederick Watson in 1933. "It would seem to be
. . . a kind of literary infection. It is, one may suggest, the genius
not only for creating comic characters like Jorrocks, but for enabling
the reader to partake of their exuberance, share their adventures,
and echo their tremendous gusts of laughter. Surtees possessed im-
aginative energy. Not only do his characters live, but, what is just as
important, they *revel* in the fact, and this zest for life, whether in
the hunting-field or in the dealer's yard, whether in a horse or in a
host, is really what matters in the end."23

From the perspective of 1968, Mr. Bonamy Dobrée assessed the
contribution of the writer who had been dead just a little over a century.

It would be absurd to claim for him a rank equal to that of Dickens and
Thackeray; but it is fair to say that he established a realm of his own. . . .
What he did contribute . . . was an enlargement of the field of the novel,
bringing in a whole new section of society, not only the followers of
hounds—numerous and varied enough—but the small country dweller, the
farmer, people whose interests were entirely local, as his mainly were. It
was the manner of life of such people, their idiosyncrasies, that he enjoyed
depicting. . . . Surtees, one feels it at every point, had more than the
mere novelist's eye that suffices the second-rate novelist; he had the
knowledge that comes from an active interest in the doings of men.24

Mr. Charles Alva Hoyt, in 1967, had similar words of praise for Surtees and ended his essay on a note echoed by modern Surteesians:

Robert Smith Surtees is a neglected author to whom our century might very well look both for entertainment and instruction. To be sure Surtees is a minor novelist, in the most accepted sense of the term: he is a specialist, a sporting writer, and the best in our language. . . . A British sporting writer then, if he is a good one, will have a great deal to say about his time. Surtees was the best, and his opinions of nineteenth-century British society are both wise and diverting: vigorous, unsparing, almost always highly critical. His irony is intense, his indignation warm, although he frequently melts into long passages of sheer fun, and nonsense, that sole delight among Victorian writers. For these and other reasons he remains easy to read; I find him one of the most congenial of the nineteenth century novelists. [25]

Notes and References

Chapter One

1. Frederick Watson, *Robert Smith Surtees: A Critical Study* (London, 1933), p. 13.

2. Robert Smith Surtees, Memoirs, edited by E. D. Cuming, *Robert Smith Surtees: Creator of "Jorrocks" by Himself and E. D. Cuming* (New York, 1924), p. 60. Hereafter, when Surtees's own notes are quoted, referred to as Surtees, Memoirs.

3. Leonard Cooper, *R. S. Surtees* (London, 1952), p. 16.

4. Robert Smith Surtees, *Plain or Ringlets* (London, 1860), p. 187.

5. Surtees, Memoirs, p. 13.

6. Surtees, *Plain*, p. 186.

7. Surtees, *Plain*, pp. 143 - 144.

8. Robert Smith Surtees, *Analysis of the Hunting Field* (London, 1846), p. 154.

9. Charles Apperley (Nimrod), "Nimrod's Northern Tour," *New Sporting Magazine* (1938), as quoted by Watson, p. 23.

10. Robert Smith Surtees, "Description of Durham" (1861), as quoted by E. D. Cuming, *Robert Smith Surtees: Creator of "Jorrocks" by Himself and E. D. Cuming* (New York, 1924), p. 172.

11. Surtees, Memoirs, p. 7.

12. Cooper, pp. 16 - 17.

13. Surtees, Memoirs, p. 8.

14. Robert Smith Surtees, *Mr. Sponge's Sporting Tour* (London, 1852), p. 262.

15. Robert Smith Surtees, *Hillingdon Hall* (London, 1888), p. 313.

16. Cooper, p. 14.

17. Susan Alice Hallgarth, "Robert Smith Surtees: A Critical Reevaluation," Unpublished Ph.D. Dissertation (University of Missouri, August 1967), p. 30.

18. David Johnston-Jones, *The Deathless Train: The Life and Work of Robert Smith Surtees*, Salzburg Studies in English Literature (Salzburg, 1974), p. 7, note 2.

19. Robert Smith Surtees, *Young Tom Hall*, E. D. Cuming, ed. (London, 1926), chapters 14, 15.

20. Cooper, p. 21.

21. Cuming, p. 132

22. Cooper, pp. 25 - 26.

23. Surtees, *Plain*, p. 141.

24. Robert Smith Surtees, *Ask Mamma* (Bath, 1926), p. 420.
25. Surtees, *Hillingdon*, p. 190.
26. Robert Smith Surtees, *Handley Cross* (Bath, 1926), p. 166.
27. Surtees, *Handley*, p. 175.
28. Cooper, p. 34.
29. Robert Smith Surtees, *Jorrocks' Jaunts and Jollities* (London, 1949), pp. 9, 11.
30. J. G. . Lockhart, "*Handley Cross; or, the Spa Hunt,*" *Quarterly Review*, LXXI (March 1843), p. 392.
31. Surtees, *Handley*, p. 56.
32. Aubrey Noakes, *Horses, Hounds and Humans: ·Being the Dramatized Story of R. S. Surtees* (London, 1957), p. 81.
33. Watson, p. 227.
34. Surtees, Memoirs, p. 29.
35. Robert Smith Surtees, *Hawbuck Grange* (Bath, 1926), p. 127.
36. Surtees, *Handley*, pp. 16 - 17.
37. Surtees, Memoirs, p. 31.
38. Surtees, *Hawbuck*, p. 215.
39. Surtees, *Plain*, Chapters 50, 56.
40. Surtees, Memoirs, pp. 39 - 40.
41. Surtees, Memoirs, p. 60.
42. Surtees, Memoirs, p. 60.
43. Frederick J. Harvey Darton, *From Surtees to Sassoon: Some English Contrasts* (London, 1831), p. 10.
44. Surtees, Memoirs, p. 61.
45. Cuming, p. 115.
46. Cuming, p. 123.
47. Watson, p. 54.
48. Watson, p. 58.
49. Noakes, p. 69.
50. Watson, p. 139.
51. Surtees, *Hawbuck*, p. 222.
52. Hallgarth, p. 18.
53. Watson, p. 170.
54. Surtees, *Analysis*, p. 13.
55. Robert Smith Surtees, *Town and Country Papers*, E. D. Cuming, ed. (London, 1929), p. 208.
56. Robert Smith Surtees, *Mr. Romford's Hounds* (Bath, 1926), p. 162.
57. Hallgarth, p. 20.
58. Surtees, *Romford*, p. 52.
59. Moira O'Neill, "Some Novels by Surtees," *Blackwood's Magazine*, CXCIII (April 1913), p. 536.
60. Hallgarth, p. 19.
61. Hallgarth, p. 19.
62. Surtees, *Jaunts*, p. 15.
63. Lockhart, p. 411.

64. *Sunday Times* (London, 1843), as quoted by Cooper, p. 73.

65. Surtees, Memoirs, p. 62.

66. Surtees, Memoirs, p. 118.

67. Surtees, Memoirs, p. 143.

68. O'Neill, p. 537.

69. Alex Hamilton, Introduction to *Jorrocks' Jaunts and Jollities* by R. S. Surtees, The First Novel Library (London, 1968), p. viii.

70. Cooper, p. 59.

71. Surtees, Memoirs, p. 85.

72. Cuming, p. 131.

73. Noakes, p. 30.

74. Surtees, Memoirs, p. 106.

75. Surtees, Memoirs, p. 143.

76. Cooper, pp. 45 - 46.

77. Darton, p. 19.

78. Cuming, p. 140.

79. Surtees, Memoirs, p. 208.

80. Watson, p. 86.

81. Surtees, Memoirs, pp. 148 - 149.

82. Cuming, p. 152.

83. Watson, p. 175.

84. Surtees, *Plain*, p. 46.

85. Hallgarth, p. 25.

86. Hamilton, pp. ix - x.

87. Surtees, *Sponge*, p. 50.

88. Surtees, *Romford*, p. 219.

89. Surtees, *Romford*, p. 217.

90. Surtees, *Romford*, p. 174.

91. Surtees, *Romford*, p. 186.

92. Surtees, *Sponge*, p. 50.

93. Surtees, *Plain*, p. 194.

94. Surtees, Memoirs, p. 71.

95. Noakes, p. 116.

96. Surtees, *Plain*, p. 62.

97. Surtees, *Plain*, p. 398.

98. W. L. Renwick, "Jorrocks: A Conversation," *Essays and Studies*, XVII:17 (Oxford, 1932), p. 82.

99. Surtees, *Handley*, pp. 235 - 236.

100. Surtees, Memoirs, p. 199.

101. Surtees, Memoirs, p. 200.

102. Surtees, Memoirs, p. 227.

103. Cooper, pp. 64 - 65.

104. Surtees, Memoirs, p. 271.

105. Surtees, *Analysis*, Preface. Future page references to this title, in this section, appear in the text.

106. Darton, p. 24.
107. Cooper, p. 60.
108. Surtees, Memoirs, p. 295.
109. Surtees, Memoirs, p. 300.
110. Surtees, Memoirs, p. 328.
111. E. W. Boville, *The England of Nimrod and Surtees*, 1815 - 1854 (London, 1959), p. 27.
112. Surtees, Memoirs, p. 317.
113. Cooper, pp. 158 - 159.

Chapter Two

1. The titles of the stories which constitute *Jorrocks' Jaunts and Jollities* are as follows: "The Swell and the Surrey," "The Yorkshireman and the Surrey," "Surrey Shooting: Mr. Jorrocks in Trouble," "Mr. Jorrocks and the Surrey Staghounds," "The Turf: Mr. Jorrocks at Newmarket," "A Week at Cheltenham," "Aquatics: Mr. Jorrocks at Margate," "The Road: English and French," "Mr. Jorrocks in Paris," "Sporting in France," "A Ride to Brighton," "Mr. Jorrocks' Dinner-Party," "The Day After the Feast."
2. Surtees, *Jorrocks*, pp. 76 - 78. Further page references to this novel, in this section, appear in the text.
3. Surtees, Memoirs, p. 78.
4. Watson, p. 67.
5. Surtees, *Jorrocks*, 2nd edition, Preface.
6. Surtees, *Handley*, Preface. Further page references to this novel, in this section, appear in the text.
7. Watson, p. 32.
8. Hallgarth, pp. 74 - 75.
9. Hallgarth, pp. 81 - 82.
10. Surtees, Memoirs, pp. 280 - 281.
11. Cooper, p. 60.
12. Cooper, p. 89.
13. Cooper, pp. 89 - 90.
14. Hallgarth, p. 68.
15. Watson, p. 223. Internal quotation from Esmé Wingfield-Stratford, *The Victorian Tragedy* (London, 1930), p. 224.
16. Surtees, Memoirs, p. 12.
17. Surtees, Memoirs, p. 88.
18. Watson, p. 68.
19. Watson, p. 152.
20. Johnston-Jones, p. 48.
21. O'Neill, p. 540.
22. Watson, p. 46.
23. Watson, p. 68.
24. Noakes, pp. 85, 88.

25. W. C. Rivers, "The Place of R. S. Surtees," *The London Mercury*, X (October 1925), p. 607.
26. Watson, p. 105.
27. Siegfried Sassoon, Introduction to *Hunting Scenes from Surtees*, Lionel Gough, ed. (London, 1953), p. xii.
28. Rivers, p. 610.
29. "Robert Smith Surtees," *Times Literary Supplement* (March 27, 1930), p. 257.
30. Surtees, *Hillingdon*, p. 32. Further page references to this novel, in this section, appear in the text.
31. Hallgarth, pp. 88 - 89.
32. Noakes, p. 94.
33. Cuming, p. 225.
34. Noakes, p. 157.
35. Watson, p. 105.
36. Surtees, Memoirs, p. 168.
37. Cooper, p. 76.
38. Watson, p. 104.
39. Noakes, pp. 103 - 104.

Chapter Three

1. Surtees, *Hawbuck*, p. 237. Further page references to this novel, in this section, appear in the text.
2. Renwick, p. 86.
3. Cooper, p. 104.
4. Cooper, p. 105.
5. Noakes, p. 106.
6. Surtees, Memoirs, pp. 308 - 309.
7. Cooper, p. 106.
8. Sassoon, p. ix.
9. Watson, p. 166.
10. Cooper, p. 107.
11. Watson, p. 158.
12. Cooper, pp. 104 - 105.
13. Hallgarth, p. 51.
14. Watson, p. 198.
15. Watson, p. 198.
16. Surtees, *Sponge*, Preface. Further page references to this novel, in this section, appear in the text.
17. Watson, p. 199.
18. Watson, p. 201.
19. Noakes, p. 109.
20. Johnston-Jones, p. 155.
21. Watson, p. 203.

22. Noakes, p. 111.
23. Watson, p. 204.
24. Watson, p. 204.
25. Watson, p. 200.
26. Hallgarth, p. 104.
27. Cooper, p. 109.
28. Surtees, Memoirs, p. 263.
29. Cuming, p. 323.
30. O'Neill, p. 541.
31. Surtees, Memoirs, p. 274.

Chapter Four

1. Darton, p. 18.
2. Surtees, Memoirs, p. 61.
3. Cuming, p. 216.
4. Surtees, *Town and Country Papers*, p. 65.
5. Surtees, *Hawbuck*, p. 238.
6. Surtees, *Hall*, p. x. Further page references to this novel, in this section, appear in the text.
7. Cuming, Introduction to *Hall*, p. x.
8. Cooper, p. 114.
9. Noakes, p. 124.
10. Cooper, p. 115.
11. William Harrison Ainsworth, letter to Surtees, quoted by Cuming in *Hall*, p. 359.
12. Cuming, Introduction to *Hall*, p. xii.
13. Hallgarth, p. 49.
14. Hallgarth, p. 135.
15. Noakes, p. 129.
16. Cooper, p. 129.
17. Cooper, p. 129.
18. Johnston-Jones, pp. 45 - 46.
19. Ainsworth, *Hall*, p. x.
20. Cooper, p. 128.
21. Cuming, Introduction to *Hall*, p. xi.
22. Hamilton, p. xiv.
23. Hallgarth, p. 134.
24. Cuming, Introduction to *Hall*, p. xii.
25. Surtees, *Hall*, p. 1.
26. Surtees, *Ask*, p. 34. Further page references to this novel, in this section, appear in the text.
27. Surtees, *Hall*, p. 4.
28. Surtees, *Hall*, p. 5.
29. Surtees, *Hall*, p. 2.

30. Hallgarth, p. 48.
31. Watson, p. 254.
32. Hallgarth, p. 124.
33. Cooper, p. 126.
34. Cooper, p. 88.
35. Surtees, "Description of Durham," as quoted by Cuming, p. 159.
36. Cooper, pp. 131 - 132.
37. Surtees, "Description of Durham," as quoted by Cuming, p. 157.
38. Cooper, p. 133.
39. Noakes, p. 142.
40. Hallgarth, p. 143.
41. Surtees, *Plain*, p. 368. Further page references to this novel, in this section, appear in the text.
42. Cooper, p. 134.
43. Cooper, p. 136.
44. Cooper, pp. 134 - 135.
45. Cooper, p. 134.
46. Cooper, p. 124.
47. Cooper, p. 134.
48. Cooper, p. 135.
49. Noakes, p. 145.
50. Cooper, pp. 147 - 148.
51. Hallgarth, pp. 148 - 149.

Chapter Five

1. Cooper, p. 150.
2. Surtees, *Sponge*, p. 346.
3. Surtees, *Sponge*, p. 399.
4. Surtees, *Sponge*, p. 346.
5. Surtees, *Romford*, pp. 6 - 7. Further page references to this novel, in this section, appear in the text.
6. Watson, pp. 145 - 146.
7. Noakes, p. 149.
8. "The Novels of Surtees," *Times Literary Supplement* (December 28, 1916), p. 632.
9. Rivers, pp. 609 - 610.
10. Cooper, p. 14.
11. Surtees, *Handley*, p. 197.
12. Cooper, p. 15.
13. Surtees, *Hillingdon*, p. 108.
14. Surtees, *Hillingdon*, p. 108.
15. Surtees, *Hillingdon*, pp. 93 - 94.
16. Surtees, *Hillingdon*, p. 104.
17. Cooper, p. 66.
18. Cooper, p. 153.

19. Watson, p. 217.

20. Surtees, *Sponge*, p. 365.

21. Johnston-Jones, pp. 157 - 158.

Chapter Six

1. Theodore Roosevelt, 1906, as quoted by Watson, pp. 270 - 271.

2. Sassoon, p. x.

3. Una Pope-Hennessey, *Durham Company* (London, 1914), p. 220.

4. Cuming, p. 245.

5. Cuming, p. 260.

6. Pope-Hennessey, p. 205.

7. Siegfried Sassoon, *The Complete Memoirs of George Sherston: Memoirs of a Fox-Hunting Man* (London, 1937), p. 119.

8. Sassoon, *Hunting Scenes*, p. ix.

9. Rudyard Kipling, "My Son's Wife," *The Best Short Stories of Rudyard Kipling*, Randall Jarrell, ed. (Garden City, New York, 1961), p. 550.

10. Kipling, p. 555.

11. Arthur Quiller-Couch, as quoted by Cooper, p. 148.

12. George Saintsbury, *The English Novel* (London, 1913), p. 257.

13. O'Neill, p. 535.

14. "Sporting Literature," *Fraser's Magazine*, XVIII (October 1838), pp. 481, 488, 482.

15. Lockhart, pp. 395, 411.

16. Ernest A. Baker, *History of the English Novel: The Age of Dickens and Thackeray* (London, 1934 - 1935), VII:230.

17. Watson, pp. 244 - 245.

18. O'Neill, p. 535.

19. Cooper, pp. 166 - 167.

20. Cooper, p. 168.

21. Virginia Woolf, *Common Reader* (New York, 1948), p. 135.

22. Cooper, p. 163.

23. Watson, p. 271.

24. Bonamy Dobrée, "Robert Smith Surtees," *Imagined Worlds*, Maynard Mack, ed. (London, 1968), pp. 157, 160, 170.

25. Charles Alva Hoyt, "Robert Smith Surtees," *Minor British Novelists*, C. A. Hoyt, ed. (Carbondale, Illinois, 1967), pp. 59 - 60.

Selected Bibliography

PRIMARY SOURCES

There have been several editions of the complete novels of Robert Smith Surtees: one of the best known is the Methuen collection (complete except for *Hillingdon Hall* and *Young Tom Hall*), published in 1916; and another is the ten-volume Eyre and Spottiswoode collection, published in 1930. Currently the ten-volume *Novels of Surtees*, reprints of the 1930 edition, is available from AMS Press. Below are listed the complete works of Surtees, including nonfiction as well as fiction.

Analysis of the Hunting Field. London: Rudolph Ackermann, 1846.

Ask Mamma, or the Richest Commoner in England. London: Bradbury and Agnew, 1858.

Handley Cross, or the Spa Hunt. London: Henry Colburn, 1843.

Hawbuck Grange, or the Sporting Adventures of Thomas Scott, Esq. London: Longmans, 1847.

Hillingdon Hall, or the Cockney Squire. London: Henry Colburn, 1845.

Hints to Railway Travelers and Country Visitors to London. London: Bradbury and Evans, 1852.

Horseman's Manual. London: Alfred Miller, 1831.

Hunting Scenes from Surtees. Lionel Gough, ed. London: Rupert Hart-Davis, 1953.

Hunting Tours of Surtees. E. D. Cuming, ed. London: Blackwood and Son, 1927.

Jorrocks' Jaunts and Jollities. London: Walter Spiers, 1838.

Mr. Facey Romford's Hounds. London: Bradbury and Evans, 1865.

Mr. Sponge's Sporting Tour. London: Bradbury and Agnew, 1853.

Plain or Ringlets. London: Bradbury and Evans, 1860.

Shooting with Surtees. Hugh S. Gladstone, ed. New York: Fredrick A. Stokes, 1928.

Thoughts on Hunting and Other Matters. E. D. Cuming, ed. London: Blackwood and son, 1925.

Town and Country Papers. E. D. Cuming, ed. London: Blackwood and Son, 1929.

Young Tom Hall, his Heart-aches and Horses. E. D. Cuming, ed. London: Blackwood and Son, 1926.

160

SECONDARY SOURCES

1. Books

BOVILLE, E. W. *The England of Nimrod and Surtees*, 1815 - 1854. London: Oxford University Press, 1959. A very readable picture of English society at the time of Surtees, with brief biographies of Nimrod and Surtees and an analysis of their relationship.

COLLISON, ROBERT L. *A Jorrocks Handbook*. London: Coole Book Service, 1964. A dictionary of terms, people, and places appearing in the Jorrocks books.

COOPER, LEONARD. *R. S. Surtees*. London: Arthur Barker, 1952. A critical biography of Surtees especially helpful for its comments concerning the relationship between Surtees's life and his works.

CUMING, E. D. *Robert Smith Surtees: Creator of "Jorrocks" by Himself and E. D. Cuming*. New York: Charles Scribner's Sons, 1924. The original publication of the completed fragments of Surtees's memoirs along with many Surtees letters and commentary by Mr. Cuming.

DARTON, FREDRICK J. HARVEY. *From Surtees to Sassoon: Some English Contrasts*. London: Morley and Mitchell Kennerley Jr., 1931. An investigation of the literature of sport devoting primarily one chapter to fairly general comments about Surtees.

HAMILTON, ALEX. Introduction to Surtees's *Jorrocks' Jaunts and Jollities*. The First Novel Library Series. London: Cassell, 1968. Some original evaluations and opinions concerning not just *Jaunts* but all Surtees's works.

JOHNSTON-JONES, DAVID. *The Deathless Train: The Life and Work of Robert Smith Surtees*. Salzburg Studies in English Literature. Salzburg: Instut fur Englische Sprache und Literatur, 1974. Originally written as a dissertation, it is more valuable as a summary of previous Surtees research than for original interpretation.

NOAKES, AUBREY. *Horses, Hounds and Humans: Being the Dramatized Story of R. S. Surtees*. London: Oldbourne, 1957. A chatty, informal book that recaps to a great extent the works of Cuming, Watson, and Cooper; not much original here, but very readable.

POPE-HENNESSEY, UNA. *Durham Company*. London: Chatto and Windus, 1914. One chapter devoted to Surtees contains author's personal impressions of Hamsterley and usual biographical information.

STEEL, ANTHONY. *Jorrocks's England*. New York: E. P. Dutton, 1932. A sociological study of the England of Surtees's day using Surtees's descriptions as a basis for analysis.

TROLLOPE, ANTHONY. *British Sports and Pastimes*. London: Virtue, 1868. Shows Surtees and the subjects of his books through the perspective of one of his critical contemporaries.

WATSON, FREDERICK. *Robert Smith Surtees: A Critical Study.* London: George G. Harrap, 1933. A major work on Surtees, it builds on Cuming's work by analyzing much of the sporting scene in England during Surtees's time, discussing such things as Surtees's view of the Master of Fox-Hounds, of huntsmen, of women, of farmers, etc.

2. Articles and Essays

BAKER, ERNEST A. *History of the English Novel.* Vol. VII: *The Age of Dickens and Thackeray.* New York: Barnes and Noble, 1936. Discussion of Surtees as representative of his age.

CHILD, HAROLD. "Caricature and the Literature of Sport." *Cambridge History of English Literature,* Vol. 14. New York: G. P. Putnam's Sons, 1917. Puts the works of Surtees into the context of similar writings by his contemporaries.

DOBRÉE, BONAMY. "Robert Smith Surtees." *Imagined Worlds.* Maynard Mack ed. London: Methuen, 1968. Evaluation of the place of Surtees in development of English literature.

HOYT, CHARLES ALVA. "Robert Smith Surtees." *Minor British Novelists.* C. A. Hoyt, ed. Carbondale, Illinois: Southern Illinois University Press, 1967. Review of Surtees's novels with emphasis on his contribution to English literature.

LOCKHART, J. G. "Handley Cross; or, the Spa Hunt." Quarterly Review. LXXI (March 1843), pp. 392 - 411. Review of the novel following its original publication.

"Novels of Surtees." *Times Literary Supplement* (December 28, 1916), p. 632. A review of Surtees's novels upon the release of the Methuen editions.

O'NEILL, MOIRA. "Some Novels by Surtees." *Blackwood's Magazine.* CXCIII (April 1913), pp. 535 - 542. Personal thoughts by a Surtees admirer.

RENWICK, W. L. "Jorrocks: A Conversation." *Essays and Studies,* XVII:17. Oxford: Clarendon Press, 1932. Cast as an argument between friends on the value of reading Surtees, this creative and humorous article covers the main criticism of Surtees's works, pro and con.

RIVERS, W. C. "The Place of R. S. Surtees." *The London Mercury.* X (October 1924), pp. 605 - 613. A short but scholarly evaluation of Surtees's novels.

"Robert Smith Surtees." *Times Literary Supplement* (March 27, 1930), pp. 257 - 258. Criticism of Eyre and Spottiswoode edition of Surtees's novels and of the novels themselves.

3. Dissertation

HALLGARTH, SUSAN. "Robert Smith Surtees: A Critical Re-evaluation." Unpublished Ph.D. Dissertation for the University of Missouri, August 1967. An excellent work providing new ways of evaluating the literary techniques employed by Surtees in his novels as well as interesting opinions on his individual works.

Index

Ackermann, Rudolph, 26
Adam Bede (Eliot), 147
Ainsworth, William Harrison, 102 - 104, 108, 147
Apperley, Charles James. (See "Nimrod")
"Ask Mamma Polka," 144
Austen, Jane, 122

Beckford, William, 149
Bell, William, 18
Bell's Life, 35, 84
Bennett, Arnold, 143
Birkett, James, 16 - 17
Boulogne, 30, 42, 46, 61, 86, 123
Brighton, 21, 23, 37, 40, 123
Bronte(s), Charlotte and Emily, 122, 147
Byron, George Gordon, Lord, 122

Carleton, J. W., 29
Chapman, George, 58
Characterization, 23 - 25, 103, 108 - 12, 119, 126, 138 - 41, 148, 150; based on real people (See Satire, of real people); Glitters, 94, 113, 138, 140 - 41; Hall, 104, 109 - 12; Jorrocks, 20 - 21, 26 - 27, 40, 45, 47, 54, 57 - 60, 69 - 71, 146; McDermott, 119; Mainchance, 113 - 16; minor characters, 61, 64, 89 - 91, 95 - 98 , 108 - 109, 112 - 13, 119; Pigg, 62 - 63; Pringle, 109 - 12; Romford, 135 - 36; Scott, 80 - 84; Sponge, 87 - 88, 90 - 91, 94 - 95, 104
Cheltenham, 40
Cloister and the Hearth, The, (Reade), 147
"Cockney," 19 - 21, 40, 42, 44 - 45, 48, 50 - 51, 60, 65 - 66, 69, 79, 144
Colburn, Henry, 57
Cooper, Abraham, 26

Corn Laws, 34 - 35, 69, 76 - 78

Dickens, Charles, 57 - 58, 88, 143 - 45, 147 - 48, 150
Dixon, Scarth, 62
Durham County. (See Hamsterley)
Durham Grammar School, 17

Elcho, Lord, 99 - 100
Eld, Captain, 21
Eliot, George, 147
Encyclopaedia of Rural Sports (Blaine), 37

Falstaff, 55, 57 - 58
Fenwick, Addison, 33
Fenwick, Elizabeth Jane. (See Surtees, Elizabeth Jane)
Field, 37, 144
Fielding, Henry, 30
Flyers of the Hunt (Mill), 146
Framley Parsonage (Trollope), 147
France, 18, 21, 63

Gablenz, Baron, 21, 86, 123
Gaskell, Elizabeth, 88, 147
Great Expectations (Dickens), 147
Greville, Charles Cavendish Fulke, 29
Greville Diaries, The (Greville), 73

Hamsterley, (Durham County), 13 - 19, 22 - 23, 27 - 28, 33 - 38, 56, 73, 76, 85, 114, 138, 146
Harriers, 15, 71, 84 - 85
Herne Bay, 40 - 41, 46
Hunting, as satiric norm, 15 - 16, 20 - 21, 24, 44 - 45, 54, 56, 84 - 85, 104; importance of, 14 - 15, 22, 33, 44; morality of (incl. other sports), 22 - 23, 30 - 33, 35
Hunting Scenes from Surtees, 66, 145

Ingham, Robert, 81

Jane Eyre (Bronte), 122
Jonson, Ben, 58

Keats, John, 122
Kipling, Rudyard, 145
Kirk, Josh, 62

Lambton, Ralph, 15 - 16, 18, 29, 33, 37, 84, 100
Leech, John, 36, 38, 57, 100, 143 - 44, 146
Lytton, Edward Bulwar, 147

Margate, 40 - 42, 45
Martin, Richard, 30
Mill, James, 146
Mill on the Floss, The (Eliot), 147
"My Son's Wife" (Kipling), 145

Narrative method, 40, 46 - 47, 50, 54 - 57, 72 - 76, 80, 85 - 87, 95, 99 - 100, 103, 109, 114 - 15, 117 - 19, 124 - 26, 131 - 32, 141 - 42
New Market, 23, 40 - 43, 46, 146
New Monthly Magazine, 37, 102 - 103
New Sporting Magazine, 26 - 27, 32, 35, 40, 42, 45 - 46, 56 - 57, 142, 144, 146
Newcastle, 14, 17 - 19
"Nimrod" (Charles James Apperley), 15, 22 - 23, 25 - 26, 34, 37, 42, 48 - 49, 57, 63 - 64, 83, 102, 149
Northumberland, 73

Ovingham, 16 - 17

Paris, 23, 34, 40, 43, 46 - 47
Pickwick, 57 - 58
Poor Laws, 38
Posthumous Papers of the Pickwick Club, The (Dickens), 144, 146
Purvis, Robert, 17

Quixote, 55

Raleigh, Walter, 124
Reade, Charles, 88
Roosevelt, Theodore (Mr. & Mrs.), 143

Sassoon, Siegfried, 81, 143 - 45
Satire, 20 - 21, 44 - 45, 98 - 99, 112, 119, 125, 136 - 37; from personal experience, 19, 21, 23, 30, 34 - 36, 40 - 45, 69, 76 - 78, 85 - 86; method, 17, 23 - 25, 40, 47, 49 - 50, 56, 64 - 65, 71, 89 - 91, 103 - 109, 131 - 32, 136; of actual places, 21, 23, 37, 40 - 43; of doctors, 48 - 49, 64 - 65; of foreigners, 21, 49, 86, 123 - 24; of law and lawyers, 19, 49, 53 - 55, 64 - 65, 68 - 69; of pseudo-gentry, 48, 64 - 65, 89, 91 - 92, 114 - 16, 123, 137; of real people, 16 - 17, 21, 25, 61 - 64, 73, 86, 108, 123 - 24, 144; of soldiers, 18, 34, 86, 107 - 108
Scott, Walter, 122
Seymour, Robert, 144
Sholbert, William, 57, 81
Shotley Bridge, 21
Smollett, Tobias, 30, 58
Sporting Magazine, 22, 25 - 26, 29
Sterne, Laurence, 58, 85 - 86
Subscription packs, 19 - 20, 44 - 45
Surtees, Anthony (brother), 27
Surtees, Anthony (father), 14 - 15, 18, 22, 27 - 29, 85
Surtees, Anthony (son), 36
Surtees, Eleanor, 36
Surtees, Elizabeth Anne, 36
Surtees, Elizabeth Jane (Fenwick), 33, 113
Surtees, Robert Smith (1805 - 1864), community service, 34, 36, 38; description of, 28; domestic life, 13 - 14, 28 - 29, 33 - 34, 36, 39; early years, 13 - 17; editor, 26 - 27, 37; education, 16 - 17; hunting correspondent, 18, 22 - 27, 35, 37; law, 17 - 19, 21 - 22, 27; politics, 29 - 30, 34 - 35

WORKS - FICTION:
Ask Mamma, 19, 37, 48, 76, 81, 103, 109 - 19, 122, 124, 131, 147
Handley Cross, 19 - 21, 25, 27, 35 - 36, 48, 50 - 66, 67, 70 - 72, 79, 84, 87, 91, 94 - 95, 100 - 101, 108, 116, 134, 141, 143 - 47, 150

Hawbuck Grange, 21, 23, 36, 75, 79 -
   87, 100, 102, 118
Hillingdon Hall, 17, 19, 21, 30, 34 - 35,
   48, 57, 64, *66 - 78,* 79, 85, 100 - 101,
   115 - 16, 118 - 19, 13, 139, 147
Jorrocks' Jaunts and Jollities, 19 - 20, 25,
   27, 35, *40 - 50,* 51, 53, 64, 67, 72, 79,
   144, 149, 155n1
Mr. Romford's Hounds, 24, 31, 37 - 38,
   93, 119, *126 - 42,* 143, 149
Mr. Sponge's Sporting Tour, 16 - 17, 27,
   31 - 33, 36, 87 - 100, 102, 108, 125 -
   28, 134, 141, 143 - 44, 146
Plain or Ringlets, 13 - 14, 19, 21, 30, 32 -
   33, 37, 49, 103, 116, *119 - 25,* 131,
   147
Young Tom Hall, 34, 37, *101 - 109,* 110 -
   12, 118 - 19, 122, 126

WORKS - NON-FICTION:
Analysis of the Hunting Field, 15, 24,
   35 - 36

"Breaking Ground," 22 - 23
"Description of Durham," 15, *36 - 37,*
   76, 114 - 15
Horseman's Manual, 27, 101
Hunting Tours, 20
*Robert Smith Surtees, by Himself and E.
   D. Cuming* (Memoirs), 38
Town and Country Papers, 24

Tennyson, Alfred, 147
Thackeray, William Makepeace, 38 - 39,
   143 - 44, 147, 150
Trastram Shandy (Sterne), 85

Whyte-Melville, 147
Windham, Colonel, 21
Woolf, Virginia, 149 - 50
Wuthering Heights (Bronte), 122